To Wesley
on your wedding day

God Bless you on
your journey to
Become One —

Barbara Del Buono
and
Tom Del Buono

WHEN TWO BECOME ONE

The Miracle in Marriage

Also by Barbara Del Buono

ACKNOWLEDGED A MAN

Survivor of Assault in the YMCA

COME HOLY SPIRIT

A Guide to Confirming Faith in the
Roman Catholic Church

WHEN TWO BECOME ONE

The Miracle In Marriage

by Attorney John and Barbara Del Buono

The Ellingsworth Press, L.L.C.

All rights reserved
Copyright 2000 by John and Barbara Del Buono

Published by
The Ellingsworth Press, L.L.C.

680 Main Street
Watertown, CT 06795
Telephone: 860 274-7151
Toll Free: 877 ELLPRES (355-7737)
E-mail: ELLPRESS @aol.com

No part of this book may be reproduced or transmitted in any form or by any means, electronic or mechanical, including photocopying, recording, or by any information storage and retrieval system, without permission in writing from the publisher, except in the case of brief quotations embodied in critical articles and reviews.

The paper used in this book meets the requirements of the American National Standard for Permanence of Paper for Printed Library Materials
Z39-48-1984

Publisher's Cataloging-in-publication
(Provided by Quality Books, Inc.)

Del Buono, John and Barbara
    When Two Become One: The Miracle In Marriage

Del Buono, 2nd ed. Revised

  p.cm.
  Includes index.

  Isbn: 0960569820

Second Edition Revised
        Manufactured in the United States of America

This book is dedicated to all couples
who wish to truly be *one*
and attain the happiness
from their marriage that God
intended them to have.

CREDITS:

Cover Design by

Media Vision, Michelle Smith

Photograph on front cover is of the authors on their wedding day January, 1950

Photograph on back cover is of the authors on their 50th wedding anniversary January, 2000
Courtesy of Wedding World, Nick Reynolds

CAN TWO BECOME ONE ?

If a moral and mature person
Will marry a moral and mature person
They can become one.

If a moral and mature person
Chooses to marry
an immoral and immature person
They won't become one.

If an immoral and immature person
Marries an immoral and immature person
They can't become one.

A moral person is
one who bases a lifestyle on the laws of
The Ten Commandments

A mature person is one who
can support him or herself;
maintains a high quality of love
in all aspects of life; and
gets along with other mature persons.

All persons have a God given free will
to become moral and mature.

by *John and Barbara Del Buono*

TABLE OF CONTENTS

	FOREWORD	1
Chapter		
1	COURTSHIP	9
2	WEDDING DAY	13
3	MARRIAGE	18
4	SEXUAL RELATIONS	38
5	CHILDREN	49
6	PERSONAL CHARACTER	63
7	FAMILY AND HERITAGE	78
8	RELIGION	92
9	COMMUNITY	103
10	EDUCATION	114
11	CAREER	120
12	HEALTH	128
13	FINANCES	140
14	RECREATION	149
	CONCLUSION	158

Foreword

by Attorney John Del Buono

I have been a lawyer since the year 1950. I handled divorces for thirty-five years of my career as a general practitioner. Having been happily married for fifty years, it is natural that I should want others to experience the happiness and oneness in marriage and not feel the pain associated with divorce. I had to ask myself what makes the difference between a good marriage and a bad one. What ingredients does one look for in choosing a partner that will allow for the greatest measure of success?

My overwhelming experience with marital failure has been that far too little was known about the persons attempting to live together in the most intimate relationship on earth, marriage. It is obvious that the normal safeguards of family, community, and church have been eroded away, and too much reliance has been placed on the inexperience and the impulsiveness of youth. Immaturity is an ever-present danger when young people in love decide they want to marry. How do you overcome this danger?

Unless couples learn about the whole person they are marrying there is not much chance for success. This whole person is more than the body that one can see. It involves the person's mind, emotions and spirit as well as the physical. In order to know the whole person some investigation into the mind of the partner must be made. The emotions must be explored. The spirit must be discovered. Only then can you really know the person encompassed in the body you can see.

I needed a way for couples coming into my office to receive the help they wanted and the only way of giving them assistance was to provide them with a method whereby they could learn about who it is they are trying to live with in a marriage relationship. It was then that I asked my wife, Barbara, to write this book. We decided that the only way for two people to discover who they really are is to ask them to ask questions of each other, and then let their answers reveal the true person each was trying to live with. We did not want a third party to intervene in their dialogue because we believed that each of them would know the truth of the answers the other was giving more than any one else. Further, these questions concern their private lives and should be kept between the two of them.

In using it, I have found that if both minds are open to saving the marriage each partner will be willing to go through the analysis that this book requires of them. If one person's mind is shut, then that person will not read the book with their partner, and saving the marriage is probably not possible.

Foreword

As each person reads this book, the answers to the questions it contains will reveal a fact that we have found to be true of all marriages: The level of maturity and morality in each person's life will determine the success, or failure, of their marriage to each other. That is why you will find in the front of this book the truism called, "Can Two Become One?" It has been my experience that immaturity and immorality are the greatest cause of divorce in this country today.

It behooves every person about to be married, and those already in marriage, to discover the level of maturity of yourself and the person you are married to. Without knowing this you will constantly wonder about what you are doing wrong and why you cannot get along with this person you thought you loved. Once you become educated to this fact you become free of this worry and are able to function without the guilt usually associated with a poor marriage or divorce.

As you read through the questions and answer them, a pattern will begin to emerge about yourself and your partner. You will begin to see that the level of your maturity, and the quality of your love, depends on what you think about many subjects in your life. These subjects form the chapters of this book and every one of them tells the story of your life. As you read further, you will find that maturity must be balanced with morality, and that morality will depend on whether or not you accept a code of conduct consistent with the Ten Commandments.

The Ten Commandments once were, are not now, but should again be, the basis of all of our civil and criminal laws in the United States. They are the foundation stone of every civilized society. Once these laws are repealed by government edict, citizens will be tempted to no longer obey them and consider them to be out-dated and no longer of consequence. In our beloved country the laws of the Ten Commandments began to be repealed in the 1960's and 1970's. Now it is forbidden for a list of these laws to be placed on the walls of a public school. How do the laws of the Ten Commandments affect your marriage?

Children are the natural expectation of marriage. Most couples look forward to having them. But now the power of life and death over every succeeding generation is held in the hands of one person – the mother. Abortion is no longer a crime but it does violate the moral law against killing. Therefore, the woman who conceives a child is the lone decider of whether that child will live to become a part of a new generation of people, or whether that child will die and never know what it is like to be nurtured and cared for to adulthood. Mothers alone decide who will live and who will die. In choosing a woman to marry, every man should want to know her beliefs with regard to abortion. The lives of his children are at stake in this decision. More than one and one-half million children each year are aborted in the United States since the law was changed in 1973. Abortion is not a small decision for a man and woman to make. It is of monumental importance in deciding whether or not to marry a woman who believes in abortion. The civil law will allow her to act on her belief. The moral law will not.

It is no longer a crime for your spouse to commit adultery. It used to be. It is no longer a crime to fornicate. It used to be. It is no longer a crime to work at a non-essential job on the Sabbath. It used to be. It is no longer a crime to be a vagrant and expect other working adults to support you through government programs. It used to be. It is no longer possible for a parent to sue someone for civil damages who seduces your minor daughter who was not mature enough to give her willing consent for sexual activity. It used to be. It is no longer a breach of the civil law for someone to promise to marry and then renege on that promise. It used to be. These laws, that have been repealed since the 1960's, brought stability to community life. Persons who did not obey them felt the stigma of societal disapproval because they violated not only the moral law but the civil law as well. All of them affect marriage deeply.

No longer does a child have to obey his parents until his 21st birthday. This would usually mean that the child has made a decision in conjunction with the parents about a career choice and be well on the way to having finished a college education. The extra years of maturity cannot but be helpful in the choice of a marriage partner as well. Now the child can make contracts on his or her own at the early age of 18 years without the consent of the parents. Now a young person of 18 years can choose a career and decide when and who he or she will marry without the advice and consent of the parents. This places restrictions on the parents in helping their child to make important decisions affecting his or her life that will last for a lifetime. Young persons of 18 years of age may be immature and need the guidance of the parents, but the laws no longer favor the parents and give all of the authority to the child at too early an age.

No longer is it the law that a marriage vow will be held sacred until death and that a divorce will be granted to an innocent spouse only against a guilty one. Nowadays a marriage certificate is considered a civil contract that can be breached by either party without regard to fault. Guilty spouses can get a no-fault divorce against an innocent spouse. In most states, a spouse can no longer sue a third party for alienation of affections and collect damages.

Our nation was founded on the principle of cooperation of church and state and operated this way for the most part until the 1960's. Since then this principle has been gradually changed so that the phrase "separation of church and state," contained in a letter written by Thomas Jefferson to the Danbury Baptist Association in 1802, has now become an unwritten law.

The First Amendment to our Constitution guarantees that the government cannot establish a religion that we must all follow. It in no way prohibits citizens from the free exercise of religion and following the moral laws contained in the Ten Commandments. Now, however, all three branches of the federal government impose laws on the citizens that deny them the right to have their civil laws reflect the moral law as well. It used to be that the civil and criminal laws mandated that citizens should be moral and mature by the time they reached adulthood. Present day laws in the United states favor citizens who are immoral and immature and thereby make it difficult for young people to marry persons they can trust in a marriage relationship.

These laws are invisible but real in their impact on citizens trying to choose a spouse and, when married, trying to raise a family. All persons should be aware of the impact these laws have on the relationship of partners in marriage. When the civil laws are in conflict with the moral laws of a society, some citizens may tend to believe that the moral laws are no longer to be obeyed since there is no civil or criminal penalty for violating them. This causes chaos in society and marriage in particular. It requires that those who want the oneness in marriage that God promised must live according to moral law and disregard the low standard set by government edict.

This book came about as the result of my desire to help people in troubled marriages. However, in writing the book, we found that its ideal use was for two people considering a marriage to read it with one another. And finally, we found that this book can be helpful to those in good marriages who want to know as much as possible about each other.

Men and women are distinctly sexual in their minds, emotions and spirits just as they are in their bodies. When you discover the sexuality of the person you love in all of these aspects, then, and only then, will you be able to share the greatest sexual pleasure, physically, that is possible.

A good marriage requires two very important ingredients: love and hard work. Taking either one of these for granted will bring disaster to your relationship. Read this book lovingly with your partner and go through the hard work its analysis will require of you.

There is nothing on earth that can compare with the joy of a good marriage to someone you love totally.

1

COURTSHIP

One of the most poignantly beautiful and long-remembered times in the lives of a truly happy couple is the period they look back on as their courtship. The moods, the feelings, the music, the dress, the food, even the entertainment they enjoyed together, bring forth memories that enhance their lives always. Married couples remember their courtship as a time of high romance and in no happy home does that remembrance fail to linger. It becomes sweeter and deeper as years follow upon years.

The word "courtship" is often relegated to the past but its meaning is still honorable and it does reflect the dignity and the love that justify completely the kind of anticipation that leads to a proposal of marriage and its acceptance. So, though the use of words may change, in this book we use the word "courtship" deliberately.

At no time in life are couples truly transported to "another world" as during courtship. They are allowed the pleasure and luxury of indulging each other almost without end and the world smiles with happy eyes at those in love. It is the period in our lives when we just begin to lower some of the natural, instinctive, protective barriers to knowing another person fully.

Attraction alone is enough to cause us to make some of our most private selves vulnerable to another. The manner in which we are treated during this vulnerable state determines whether the barriers will be quickly raised, or gently lowered even more. If attraction is shared, vulnerability will be forgotten and discovery will flourish. Joy and unending anticipation await those who treat each other with tenderness during this period. The romance, the joys, the anticipation of being with one another can grow into a special kind of love that provokes a feeling of wanting to be together forever. Courtship has a never-to-be-forgotten place in a happy, fulfilled married life. It should be enjoyed to the full! It should be worthy of a life-long remembrance.

Sexual attraction is an important aspect to courtship. Sex, as it pertains to the physical, is most often the attracting feature in the dating period. Yet, awareness that another is *masculine* or *feminine*, not only in the *physical* but also in the *mental*, the *spiritual* and the *emotional*, is a thrilling discovery which produces the most awesome, exciting, beautiful, eager urge "to know" that we experience.

Our relationships with our family and friends do not permit us to know the total person they are. The urge to know someone deeply, fully, totally and to be known in the same way, comes during the time when we meet someone and fall in love. The period we call courtship is the natural attempt to fulfill this need and many attempts should be made to aid us in making "the" final choice of a married partner.

Attraction on the part of only one, if pursued, leads to frustration, hurt and bewilderment about one's self. First attempts "to know" another person are as fraught with possible "accidents" as first attempts to learn to drive a car. Emotional fenders may be bent; desires may be difficult for the mind to control; injury to the spirit may occur; but these are the risks that must be taken to know and to be known.

In the midst of this courtship period other aspects of life are changing as well. Identifying one's self as an individual, distinct from family; seeking employment; establishing relationships with new friends; becoming an adult in your community and nation. These are some of the crucial lifetime decisions that we make at a time in our lives with the least maturity to make them.

One of the most deceptive aspects of courtship is the fact that two people are getting to know each other under circumstances favorable to more than a little romanticizing. Funds may be easy to come by, whether from parents or our own, and anticipation makes economy easy, even when funds are scarce. Such necessary items of life as food, clothing, shelter, and even transportation are usually minor problems and, frequently are no problem at all. Broken dates, being away for a few days, or merely having a headache, are painfully charged off to disappointment, but there is always the sustaining fact of the anticipation of being together again soon.

In married life this simply is not so. The anticipation of being together has been achieved. Life has changed. Now the necessary items of life take on huge importance. The absence of one, even for a few days, means disappointment for the other. Daily chores must be accomplished alone. Putting up with someone who simply has a headache and is no longer smiling and full of pep must be reckoned with.

To mature couples these irritations will be lovingly dealt with knowing that two lives have now become one in spirit. A married couple who learn to accept these irritations as part of their lives together begin to experience a broadening of their outlook on marriage and thereby enhance its beauty. But to those who are not mature, and who are unwilling to face the inevitable potholes along the roadways of married life, danger signals are up and disaster may lie ahead.

The transition from courtship to married life is a big one. This is one of the major reasons this book is offered to you. It is hoped that at least with some it will help make beautiful what, in so many cases, is destined to be otherwise.

2

WEDDING DAY

On your wedding day you present each other with the greatest gift either of you will ever have to offer –yourselves. Yet few brides and grooms fully realize the true nature of the gift they are giving or receiving.

No bride or groom comes to the wedding feast through his or her efforts alone. Those who cared for you through infancy, childhood, and adolescence contributed greatly to your ability to arrive at this day. These include parents, or their substitutes, neighbors in your community, teachers in your schools, ministers in your religion, friends with whom you shared your childhood and adolescence. All have had some effect on your life and have helped you to become the "gift" you now offer to your beloved. Your response to the ideas and customs these individuals imparted to you determines the person you are giving to your beloved. They could not have a greater effect on you than you would allow them to have.

The manner in which you plan your wedding day tells much about you. It will reveal the type of marriage you intend to have and the consideration you intend to give to others intimate in your lives. Weddings are infinite in their variety and varied in the amount of commitment couples make to one another.

Any time a couple engage one another in the intimate act of giving themselves to each other in sexual relations a type of marriage occurs. This type of commitment may be casual, not intended to last, but the "giving" is there nevertheless. You cannot "take" another person, or "give" yourself in this way without some commitment and consequence following. You may separate quickly thereafter but a type of marriage occurred. Neither of you will ever be the same "single" person again.

A wedding that is the result of a woman becoming pregnant is a forced affair. It may or may not include a commitment to love until death. The pressure of the pregnancy places so many doubts on the relationship that even the couple themselves may not know their true motives. If the sexual relations that resulted in the pregnancy were the result of real love between the couple, they can make a success of their marriage. Even if they were the result of real love on the part of only one, that one can make the marriage last for quite a long time through sincere effort of trying. If they were the result of passion on the part of both, the marriage is doomed to failure for both will be too selfish to make it work unless there is a real maturing after the marriage.

Couples that decide they want to live together and then do so, plan their time of commitment with little or no regard for anyone other than themselves. It is as if they were living on a planet alone. No public ceremony marking this special occasion is had. No vows are made between the two of them. Couples in this category make no acknowledgement of society, church or the laws of their community regarding marriage. They are likely to be immature in their thinking and, therefore, unable to make the kind of commitment to one another that would entail a lifelong obligation. They will never become "one" in the sense that God intended.

Couples who plan their wedding day in conjunction with the laws of society procure a marriage license and thereby state their intentions to abide by the marriage laws of their community. Such a wedding day includes a public ceremony where vows are made openly to one another. This kind of wedding ceremony may include invitations whereby family and friends are invited to share in the joy of your decision to marry. The bride and groom want their marriage to be a special occasion and want others to recognize it that way too.

The bride and groom that choose to make their commitment to love by asking the blessing of God upon their marital union, do so through the church of their religious belief. All religions have special ceremonies for joining two people in marriage. The couple who marry in the church of their religious faith are making a public affirmation of the fact that they intend to abide by the tenets of this faith and the laws of the community since the religious leader who presides at their ceremony represents both.

Most religious faiths regard marriage and the wedding vows the couple make as sacred, and in some, indissoluble until death. It will be beyond the power of any human being to know the extent of each couple's willingness to commit themselves to each other and the religious faith they are affirming. But the couple themselves will know of any reservations held and the God they acknowledge in their ceremony will also know.

So, by some reflection on the type of ceremony planned and the form of commitment made, intentions can be discerned.

Did you have a wedding ceremony?
Did a government official administer your marriage vows?
Did you intend to abide by the laws of the government that licensed you to marry?

Did a religious leader administer your marriage vows?
Were you aware of the tenets of faith of this religion?
Did you intend to live according to the tenets of faith of the religion in which you vowed to love one another until death?

Were your family and friends invited to your marriage ceremony?

Whether these people were present at your ceremony or not, their effect upon your life was there. Each husband receives the gift of wife which her parents, community and religion were able to hand to him on his wedding day. The kind of commitment they made to her, and her response to it, make up the gift he receives; no more, no less. It now becomes his commitment to take the gift given and to further help it grow. It is for this reason that the father, (representing parents, family, community and religion), gives the bride to the groom at the altar. She leaves his care and leadership for that of her husband.

And so it is for the husband too. He presents himself at the altar of marriage with the gift of self that his parents, family, community and religion were able to endow him, and his response to their efforts. The bride receives no more, and no less, than all of these people were able to present to her on this day. The groom accepts the care and leadership offered by the father of the bride and commends himself into the care of the wife, leaving his family for her, too.

3

MARRIAGE

Marriage is the oldest institution in the world. It is the way of life for most in this world of ours, even though, from time to time, its traditions change. But the institution of marriage always survives. It is the cornerstone of community living.

A good marriage is a life-long conversation with someone you come to know intimately. You constantly discover new facets in the personality of this person, this completely distinct individual, as you travel through the years together. You constantly learn of unsuspected facets in your own personality. No other relationship will bring you so close, so intimate to another human being. No other relationship will make you grow and mature as will this one.

Society desires marriages for the practical purpose of distinguishing the married from the unmarried, fixing responsibility for the rearing of children, and the orderliness that naturally develops from one man publicly vowing to take one woman to a mutual home and rearing the children that may come from their union. Most couples, however, marry for a vastly higher purpose than the practicality society desires.

The love that causes two people to marry and hope that their lives can become one, is a wonderful thing. It requires the deepest faith one can give to another human being on this earth. It brings forth vows and promises that neither can fully comprehend at the time they are made for they involve a future lifetime. It is through this kind of love and commitment that God intended the miracle of life to be passed down from one generation to the next.

These holy bonds of matrimony, lasting for a lifetime, have been enjoyed the world over century after century. Yet when we consider the solemnity of the commitment made and the unknown elements on which it is made, the astonishing fact is that so many marriages succeed and not that so many fail!

What causes some marriages to succeed and others to fail? *Love* is the cause for most people marrying, so, perhaps it is the *degree of love* that separates the successes from the failures. Love must be unequivocally shared for the marriage to last. It cannot be one-sided. Each partner must give it and receive it or the marriage will die.

What distinguishes married love from other kinds of love? There is an element of *completeness* about it that is a part of our very natures. It is what we yearn for from adolescence into adulthood. It is this kind of love that is spoken of in the Old Testament of the Bible in Genesis 2:24:

> Wherefore a man shall leave father and mother, and shall cleave to his wife, and they shall be two in one flesh.

This truth is repeated again by Jesus, centuries later, in the New Testament in St. Matthew 19: 2-4 when he says:

> Have you not read that the Creator, from the beginning, made them male and female and said, *For this cause a man shall leave his father and mother, and cleave to his wife, and the two shall become one flesh?* Therefore now they are no longer two, but one flesh. What therefore God has joined together, let no man put asunder.

God has created us male and female but it is only when we are joined as one that completeness is realized. But how does this oneness occur? What can we do to attain it?

In marriage there is an offering of the complete person: *mind, body, spirit, and emotion,* all of one's self – to one another. If there is a holding back of any part, the giving is not complete enough for the two to become one. But this total gift of self takes time to develop and grow within marriage. It is not always easy to give all of one's self, even to the beloved. One may be able to give the body, but not the spirit; the mind, but not the whole deep sweep of emotion that results in sheer ecstasy.

However, as time passes and knowledge and trust build quietly between the two, they begin to discover the true joys of total giving and to lower the barriers of their own natural, instinctive, protective defenses. This discovery does not come all at once on a wedding day. Rather, it comes slowly, soundly, in living together in marriage; while sharing the daily disappointments and triumphs; in learning that the two, talking with each other and working together, can come to a reasonable solution to any problem that confronts them *with their combined good will.*

As this attitude grows, a unity of spirit, a oneness of mind, an emotional harmony develops in the marriage resulting in tender, joyous, ecstatic physical union. This complete giving of one to the other leads the couple to the greatest amount of happiness available to man on earth. Those who experience this know it well: those who do not, sense its loss deeply.

Oneness in marriage by no means implies perfection in all things. To obtain perfect unanimity in resolving the countless problems, large and small, that all married couples encounter, is impossible. Oneness does mean unity in approach, in forbearance, in patience and in understanding.

To attain this oneness each must probe the other's thinking, for without knowing the mind of the other, unity is not possible. Their spirits must be able to soar together, traveling in the same direction, not separate ones. This delicate territory must be invaded tenderly, for the spirit is the most fragile part of any person. Each must understand the other's deepest, innermost feelings, discovering these with compassion and charity. This too, is a most vulnerable realm where one can experience the sweetest tenderness or the most piercing hurt. Only when all of this has been explored can physical union be enjoyed with the total person each married, for only then can both give all of themselves in the physical union.

The manner of becoming one in a marriage is unlike any other endeavor in the world and it requires very special considerations. It would be possible to live with almost anyone for short periods of time, to accommodate their likes and dislikes, their interests instead of yours. It is possible to like almost everyone if exposed to them only occasionally. But to live intimately in marriage with someone for a lifetime requires a different approach. It is only in marriage that people vow to live together until death parts them.

In order to fulfill this vow, married couples must know one another in depth if success is to be even a possibility. Much of the unhappiness and failure attributed to marriage is really due to the ignorance of the parties involved in knowing who they are; who they are marrying; and what they are getting into by marrying this person.

Misunderstanding and vagueness are ever-present dangers. Therefore, candor and frankness is absolutely necessary to a feeling of oneness coming about. Knowing one another totally is essential if you intend to blend your lives together in the kind of relationship that is worthy of the name marriage. Deception must be faced fairly and realistically. There is a type of self-deception that is an almost inevitable part of being human. It is understandable, even praise-worthy at times, yet it can drive a marriage to the brink of disaster and beyond if reality is forever denied.

There is a place for experts to help in all facets of married life. Seeking their distilled knowledge and applying it to your marriage when possible, or necessary, is wise and practical. But, in the last analysis, you are the expert on your marriage. No one else can live it. Your emotions, thoughts and feelings, whose intimacy you live with daily, make you the expert on how you must live your married life. Trust your own judgment and common sense; retain your own poise and self-confidence.

When you find broad agreement and only here and there "agree to disagree," then you are becoming one with each other. As you begin to understand your partner's mind, emotions, and spirit, you become one with your spouse and the physical joining as you become one in the flesh is the greatest gift God gives to a man and woman in sacred marriage. You are now enjoying the *miracle in marriage*, available only to the two of you.

MARRIAGE QUESTIONS

A marriage partner may frequently want to question their spouse about many subjects but fail to do so out of the false belief that they would be ridiculed or embarrassed if they did so. In truth there is no question that should bring about this kind of response. If it does, then the marriage may be in trouble. One of the purposes of this book is to bring up questions for you to ask each other. They require honest answers and should help you to know your spouse and yourself better.

Sometime during the course of each day every married couple should find time to just sit and talk with one another. This is essential to the health of the marriage. There is no better way to make your marriage stronger. If you are already doing this, these questions may help guide you in knowing what to talk about, or, how to bring up a subject that is on your mind.

Is being married to each other what you expected it to be?

Before you were married you had ideas about what you hoped for in the way of married life. Everyone does. Are your ideas of marriage being reasonably fulfilled? If they are, tell your partner. If they are not, say that too.

Do you agree that you spend enough time together?

One of the reasons you married was for the purpose of being together as much as possible for the rest of your lives. Have the daily routines of married life caused you to think that you were better off before you were married? Living together in the intimacy of marriage should overcome any of these feelings. If this has not happened, talk about it with your partner. You may be surprised with your spouse's response.

Do you like the way you treat each other as husband and wife?

Every married person had expectations about how they would be treated in the intimacy of married life. The roles of husband and wife have demands and rewards that no other vocation on earth brings forth. If you treat strangers with more courtesy than you do your spouse, then something is missing from your marriage and it is most often the degree of love you give and receive. Each one of you may feel that the other should sense what you are feeling and thinking. Neither of you are mind readers. Ask each other how you feel about this question.

Do you try to understand the pressures both of you have each day?

No adult gets through any day without facing some pressures. One of the most treasured gifts of marriage is that every day you can share these with a loving person who understands you better than anyone else in the world. This should relieve a lot of the pressure you feel and thereby renew you for the next day. This is something that every single person envies in a married couple.

Are you growing closer to one another since your marriage?

If you are not, then you are missing the joy that should be yours in married life. This question is probably the most important one you will answer. Your marriage is a living thing that grows day by day. If you are not growing closer to one another then you are growing apart. Feeling this kind of closeness is receiving the special love that is available only in married life. This feeling must grow until you are blended so close to one another that you are one in mind, body, spirit and emotion.

Is your marriage headed in the direction you would like it to go?

You must both want it to go in the same direction if your marriage is to go forward at all. Pulling at each other to do something the other does not want to do is selfish and disastrous. If one partner insists on a course of action the other partner does not like, then a split starts to occur that soon becomes a chasm. Talk about this with each other until you feel you are both satisfied with the direction your marriage is taking.

Are you as affectionate with each other as each of you would like to be?

Displaying affection is often a bone of contention in a marriage yet it is the easiest of all complaints to satisfy. Each of you came to this marriage from backgrounds that taught you certain rules concerning affectionate overtures. But now you are in a situation where accommodation of each other is essential. It is okay to learn new rules that suit you and your partner in your marriage.

Are you both satisfied with the place in which you live?

Your home is your retreat from the pressures of the world. It is the place where you should be the happiest. It should not be a place where there are only chores and work. It is vital that it be a place for relaxation and contentment for both of you. It should be the place you look forward to running to every day. Dissatisfaction with the place in which you live means constant discontent and resentment. Examine this question carefully for any reasons for dislike of the place in which you live. This is not an easy situation to change but talking about it with each other may make planning for a change the best possible solution.

Do you like the meals you have and are they nutritious?

Eating is one of the great pleasures of life and one we enjoy sharing with another person. Enjoying mealtime together is one of the best parts about being married. Single persons don't have this luxury in their lives and is another thing for which they envy married couples. But mealtime does not just happen. It must be planned. In most homes it is the wife that does the meal planning and cooking and it is a very important role in the marriage as it not only brings pleasure but it is the key to good health. Planning and preparing pleasing and nutritious meals is a hard job. The wife who does this should be complimented frequently for her efforts and the husband should be praised as the provider of these meals.

Do you shop and bargain for food in a manner satisfying to both of you?

As you go through these questions, the realization that a successful marriage is a lot of work should be coming to the forefront of your mind. This kind of question should make you aware of the fact that a good marriage is made up of a lot of small decisions that add up to a mountain of pleasure or pain depending on how they are decided.

Food constitutes one of the largest expenditures that most families have in their budget. Because your health is involved, it is not a place to skimp unless there is habitual extravagance. Therefore, knowing what to buy (good nutrition), knowing the best place to shop (good bargaining), preparing the food in a pleasing way (satisfying appetite) – all of these decisions are essential to the health and pleasure one should derive from the joy of eating.

Ordinarily it is the wife who shops for and prepares the food eaten in a home. It is good for her growth in maturity that she does this natural part of her role in the marriage. However, this task can be a frustrating one. Understanding the problems she faces in performing this role in the marriage is necessary to her sense of fulfillment.

In some marriages, it is the husband who prefers to do the shopping and sometimes the cooking. In the last analysis it is up to the couple to decide this but the considerations that go with performing this job are crucial.

Are you both satisfied with the manner in which you dress and the amount of money spent on clothing?

Outsiders, particularly senior families, are often amused at the remarkable change occurring in a young couple after marriage with regard to dress. Before marriage, couples dress to "attract" one another. After marriage, it is to "please" one another. There is a big difference. A husband will frequently become quite vocal regarding modesty on the part of his wife: skirts should be longer, necklines should be higher, etc. In general, a more womanly appearance replaces the previous girlish one.

Women, too, take a new interest in the manner in which their husbands dress. A wife's suggestions regarding color choices, her purchase of many items of clothing for him, her comments on what "looks nice" become welcome advice.

Couples who welcome these normal changes regarding dress benefit greatly from the addition to their lives of the masculine or feminine point of view. Properly handled it fulfills a need they have. If suggestions are resented there can be trouble. Each needs to explain their point of view to the other for understanding to take place.

Clothing is an important part of the budget too. While extravagance should be guarded against, the budget should not be so restrictive as to take the pleasure of feeling "pretty" or "handsome" out of life. With the advent of children clothing can become a real problem as finances are stretched thin and clothing seems to be a place where cuts can be made more easily than in other places. This can result in feelings of inadequacy though and couples need to discuss the prominence that clothing should take in their married life. This question should be talked about and discussed freely.

Do you plan times when you get away for a weekend alone with each other on a regular basis?

Every married couple needs the kind of emotional adrenaline that this kind of aloneness brings to the marriage. It is probably the most neglected of solutions and the most rewarding experience that a married couple can share. Your marriage is worth every effort you make to ensure its health. Getaway weekends are not only fun, they are as necessary for the health of your marriage as food is for your body.

DANGER SIGNALS

Small areas of disagreement that turn into larger ones may contain danger signals to the marriage relationship that should not be ignored. *Loving* one another is *caring*. Yet, there can come a point, even in the loving relationship of marriage, when one does not *care* any longer. Actions and words will reveal this quickly and are the clue to whether the marriage is failing.

Does either of you ever walk out of the house in anger after an argument.

If you do, you are refusing to stay and resolve whatever is bringing disagreement between you. In a marriage relationship, it is walking out on yourself. Admittedly the pain of argument with the one person who should mean the most to you can be the greatest of hurts. But it will not leave because you try to walk away from a place in which you believe the pain to be. The agony is within you and your partner. Only there can it be relieved. This is when you must become of one mind or your marriage will fail.

Does either of you ever give the other the "silent treatment?"

This form of punishment aimed at your marriage partner is very destructive to you and your spouse. It is a sign of deep-seated immaturity. It is another form of walking away from the problem in your marriage without the embarrassment or inconvenience of leaving home. It can be a worse solution than walking away because you are now just walking within. That can cause more serious problems for you, personally, than those you have with you partner.

Is either of you ever able to go to sleep with an unresolved argument between you?

If love is present in a marriage relationship, the mind will not rest until it has peace with the partner. An unresolved argument should bother you so much that you cannot sleep until a certain degree of agreement has been reached that will allow your mind to rest while you sleep. If arguments are not resolved in this manner then they will be carried over from day to day until you will be confronted with a mountain of them. Talk. Get into each other's minds and find out what is separating you. It is the only way you will save your marriage.

Does either of you ever sleep in another room, or bed, after you have argued?

This is a childish form of punishment and a real sign of immaturity. As a couple you should exercise your ability as adult human beings to discuss differences between you until some *reasonable* agreement can be reached. Actions of this type have no place in a home where couples claim to *love* one another.

Have you stopped having sexual relations for an unusually long period of time?

Sexual relations in a marriage should be the coming together of the entire person in an outward expression of unspeakable love. If this most beautiful part of your marriage is not taking place, think back to the time when it stopped. Something happened at that point in your marriage of a very serious nature. Both of you had better find out what happened and talk with each other about it. Your marriage is at stake if you do not.

Does either of you work certain hours to avoid being with the other?

If you do then you have common living quarters and share expenses but you are not living a married life. It is a sign that you are giving up on trying to have a marriage relationship with the person you professed to love until death parted you. Being together is the reason you married. Ask yourself and your partner what is wrong that you no longer have this passionate desire.

Does either of you come home from time to time and not tell the other where you have been?

In a happy home the husband and wife would not think of worrying the other in this way. When you married you agreed to give up this kind of behavior. A husband and wife have an obligation to care enough for one another not to unnecessarily cause concern to the other. Each has a right to the time of the other but it is a right that cannot be demanded. It must be freely given.

Does either of you ever strike the other in anger?

If you do, you admit that you have lost complete control of yourself. You can no longer reason with your partner so you begin to pound your point of view into your spouse. Living in a marriage relationship requires a great deal of self-control. Striking one another admits losing all of it. Never allow yourself to sink this low in your marriage relationship. If you do, it is over.

Do you ever feel that your spouse nags too much?

Nagging results from living with someone who habitually will not do the things that you believe should be done. In a marriage the partners should have such harmony of ideas on how to live that nagging will not be necessary. If this is not the case, then some accommodation of the other's point of view on how to live will have to be exercised if nagging is to be avoided. The person being nagged should examine carefully to see if there is need for change which makes the nagging justified.

Are you both willing to forgive and forget past mistakes?

It becomes very tedious living daily with someone who keeps bringing up old mistakes each time a new one occurs. Because of our human condition mistakes will be a part of our lives. Forgiveness makes this bearable. Constant dwelling on past errors is defeating of growth and kills the initiative to keep trying. Married couples who are successful constantly overlook, accommodate and forgive endless irritations, inconveniences and mistakes. But be aware that mistakes are not the same as serious breaches of faith. Those are difficult to forgive or forget and must be dealt with on a different level.

Are you both willing to make compromises when you disagree, even if it seems to mean a sacrifice of self?

Success in marriage requires each partner to constantly think of the other first. The sacrifice of self is inherent in the marriage relationship and each partner must try to please the other so long as the expectations are reasonable. Insisting on your point of view may mean getting it and then doing without the love and affection that the other attitude would develop.

Does either of you ever belittle or "put down" the other in front of friends?

This is an easy pit to fall into if you are lacking in self-confidence. It is an attempt to build your own ego rather than let your partner do that for you and you for your spouse. Each of you should be able to depend on the good will of the other for this most necessary part of being human – ego building. If you cannot, your marriage is in danger.

Putting your partner down in public may also betray a desire to talk about something that you cannot bring yourself to discuss privately. You bring it up with other people around in the hope that a discussion will ensue. However, it is wrong to inflict on others this controversy within your marriage.

Does either of you ever go on vacation alone without the other's willing consent?

To engage in this type of conduct tells your partner that you will do as you please even though you have committed yourself to your partner in marriage. It signals a desire to be single though married. No one can have the benefits of both lifestyles at the same time. Even if you try, you will lose. Vacations are a treasured part of life. Most married couples would not think of taking part in this pleasure without their spouse. If for some special reason you want to take a vacation alone you must get the willing consent of your partner or don't go.

Do you ever worry each other about whom you are with and what you are doing?

If you do, you are refusing to give that care and concern for your partner in marriage that is necessary for its life. If your partner is making unreasonable demands on your time, talk it out in a caring way. If you are spending time with someone your partner does not approve, then you had better take a look at why the person who loves you the most is concerned about this relationship.

Does either of you ever flirt with someone to make the other jealous?

Flirting with others after marriage may result in obtaining more than jealousy from the married partner. It is a dangerous game to play and clearly against the rules of married life. The cause for this desire to flirt should be discussed with your partner even though it may be difficult to do. There is some attention and love you are seeking that is not being given. Your partner has an obligation to give these to you and they should not have to be demanded in such an outrageous way.

Does either of you ever date another person?

If you do, this is a signal to all that you have given up on your marriage relationship and that its death is imminent. Is this what you want? Perhaps you should reconsider the vows that you took when you married. They do not allow for this kind of conduct.

Does either of you drink alcoholic beverages when you know it will irritate the other?

Normally there will be no irritation unless your spouse fears that too much alcohol is being consumed. One's partner can be most helpful in this matter – if allowed to be. If you have insisted on continuing to drink when your partner has asked you not to do so, have the results ever been bad? If so, you need to take a serious look at this matter and discuss it with your spouse. Your physical health may be at stake as well as the health of your marriage.

Does either of you ever feel that your work is more important to you than each other?

In a good marriage the couple never lets any issue become more important than their love for one another. Because of the necessity to work, and the satisfaction it can bring, it is easy to become obsessed with it when one enjoys what is being done. A husband or wife who feels neglected because of work should bring up this feeling and insist on talking about it. Listen and take heed for work could turn out to be the only partner you have if you do not discuss this openly and honestly.

Does either of you allow your obligations to your children to interfere with your marital happiness?

Children bring a blessing and growth to marriage that can be most satisfying and enjoyable. However, the almost constant attention they demand can present challenges and problems to a married couple that should be frequently discussed.

The commitment in marriage was to each other first. This commitment should never be neglected, even for children. If a husband or wife becomes so pre-occupied with the children that the spouse does not get proper attention then a sense of loss will occur that can never be repaired even though the children leave home. Always prepare for the time when the two of you will be alone again so that it will be as romantic as when you first married.

Does either of you feel your marriage is in danger when arguments arise regarding your children because your spouse takes their side instead of backing you up?

A particularly dangerous time in the lives of a married couple occurs when their children become teenagers. It is wise to remember that there can be many right answers to the problems of children this age. Parents can disagree and both have a right attitude. Yet they must come to a common answer as to how the problems will be handled if there is to be any peace in the home. If there is open disagreement between the parents, the child will naturally side with the parent who most nearly reflects his or her desires. If one of the parents allows this to happen, a breach between the couple will occur which can be very difficult to mend. If you habitually favor your children's point of view over that of your spouse, your marriage is in real danger.

Pay very close attention to the danger signals listed in the questions you have just answered. These are real warning signs that your marriage may not last unless you can resolve the issues between you in a caring way. Do not rob yourselves of the rewarding years that will come if you work through your problems of living in a happy marriage.

You chose this way of life because of love for another person that was overwhelming in its emotion. Draw on that love at all times to overcome any difficulties you face. It bears repeating that any problems in your lives can be solved *with your combined good will.*

When the problems in your marriage seem overwhelming, pick a time when you and your spouse can be alone and get out a photograph album and go through it. We all take pictures of our happy times together and you need to frequently look at these when some of the sad or bad times occur. They will bring back feelings that you need to recapture. They will show your love for one another. Never let it die.

4

SEXUAL RELATIONS

Physical attraction in the dating stage causes a couple to desire to know more about the person creating this powerful urge within to come to the fore. Without this physical attraction a deeper knowing might never occur.

When a couple come to know more about each other, they may begin to feel a love growing between them that is more than just physical attraction. How does this happen? By talking and talking and talking to one another. If they find that they think alike about many subjects and have similar feelings regarding many of their emotions, they may begin to feel a sense of being kindred spirits and fall in love.

This "falling in love" comes about as a result of the masculine mind exploring the feminine one and the feminine one getting to know his mind. The girl will reveal her feminine emotions to the boy and he will discover that they are distinctly unique from his masculine ones. As they discover the unique personalities of the two of them they begin to feel a sense of being lifted from this Earth because their two spirits are soaring as one in a way that does not happen with anyone else. They are experiencing sexual relations of the mind, the emotions, and the spirit. A natural desire follows to experience this on the physical level as well. It is the ultimate desire of love possessing them. Marriage is the commitment they make to one another before this ultimate desire is fulfilled. It is necessary because many consequences flow from realizing each other in the act of physical sexual relations. This act is so powerful that it can produce a child.

Much romanticizing about love is conveyed through every possible media. It is often pictured in an unreal way. Young girls are particularly susceptible to the romantic aspects of dating, often daydreaming their emotions into views of love that have little to do with reality or what the object of their affection truly feels for them. They are simply giving way to their feminine emotions that they have not yet learned to control with their minds. Their feminine instinct to be loved as a woman, complete with caring husband, home, and family, must be brought into the perspective of whether or not this type of love is possible with the young man of their dreams. Conflicts with parents may arise when a young girl believes the dream can become reality and the parents believe it cannot.

Young men, on the other hand, are very susceptible to the physical urges that accompany the dating period. Aggressive action must be a part of their role as men but in the dating period they, too, must learn to control these urges with the mind. The masculine instinct to conquer may have little to do with love and easily confuse him, as well as the object of his attraction. He may unwittingly lead the girl to believe he is conveying the kind of "love" she is dreaming about while he is only reacting to his masculine instincts. Both can become confused at this stage of the dating period and is the reason to postpone physical sex until after the time of marriage.

It is at this stage that young people should want and seek the counsel of their parents. The parents will have the knowledge of having gone through this period of life and can be of great help if the young boy and girl will allow this to happen. If the parents are fearful of any aspect of the personality they see in the person that their child has chosen to date, then the child should pay particular attention to this as his or her future life may depend on it.

Having sexual relations before a serious commitment in marriage has been made is giving in to one's emotions and ignoring all the other wonderful parts that make up the complete person. It may be satisfying for the moment, but that kind of satisfaction will not last. It is a sign that the couple is not yet mature enough to make the kind of serious commitment to one another that marriage requires. Real love demands more than an emotional high for the moment.

Loving someone totally, not just emotionally, and expressing this in physical union is one of the greatest pleasures of life. It is a powerful and desirable emotion, and for married couples, totally necessary for the health of their marriage. But it carries consequences with it to each other and to the children that may come from having sexual relations. Much damage can be done to the mind, the spirit, and the emotions if couples take advantage of physical sex without accepting the responsibilities that come with the act. Children must depend on their mothers and fathers in this regard and they are totally helpless if their parents act in an immature way regarding sex.

Sexual relations between a married couple should bring to the fore every part of the total person. It is the ultimate time when two become one as their total beings blend in one loving act. Any part withheld, for whatever reason, will be sadly felt by the other and cause the act to be less than total – less than what it could be.

Attaining the satisfaction that this type of sexual relations brings does not happen without a maturing love inter-acting between husband and wife over a considerable period of time. Couples who have been happily married for a few years know this and readily admit that their sexual relations have improved with age because their love has grown stronger and deeper with time.

Even between happily married couples, though, discussion of their sexual relations may be difficult because it is an area where complete vulnerability to being hurt is open. Yet this aspect of their lives is so important that every risk should be taken and complete openness with one another shared. Because a married couple is continually aging and their sexual relations always reflecting this change, these discussions should become a regular part of their lives.

SEXUAL RELATIONS QUESTIONS

Do you plan times together for retaining the romance in your marriage relationship?

This was a welcome joy before you were married but most couples find it a real task after marriage. Yet it was the reason you married. It is still just as important to both of you as it was before you were married so you must find time to be together in a romantic way.

If you really enjoy being together you should find time to indulge each other in the joy of companionship. If you do not enjoy time spent with each other, then you will find romance quickly fading from your marriage. Romance is what keeps your marriage alive.

With the advent of children and the care they require, it will be necessary for you to get away from home for a few days just to renew your most loving feelings for one another in a romantic way. Though children make this more difficult to do it is absolutely necessary for the health of your marriage.

Do you feel free to talk with each other about sexual relations?

Though movies and television treat this subject openly and often insensitively, you are not emotionally involved when viewing a movie or watching a television show. Within your marriage you are very personally involved and are subject to being deeply hurt. Delicacy and tenderness should be exercised in every conversation regarding your sexual relations for openness to flow.

Do you feel sexually satisfied and happy?

As husband and wife you have every right to be. Many factors may contribute to dissatisfaction but none so much as silence; the kind of silence that keeps its hurt inside when more than one person is involved in the solution. It produces heartache and misunderstanding that will prevent a change coming about.

To get the most out of your sexual relations you must insist on talking about it with your spouse until changes occur that allow you to say and feel that you are happy and satisfied in this aspect of your marriage. Love is the ingredient that will cause this to happen. It was the reason for your marriage. Sexual relations is the time when you and your beloved come together in all aspects of your life culminating in the union of two whole persons into one. A couple who love each other will make this happen.

Are you both aware that a wife is usually sexually aroused very slowly in the early years of marriage?

Now that you are married and can indulge yourselves in sexual relations at will you may discover this generalization to be true in your marriage. It requires some adjustment on the part of the husband who usually does not have this problem. He will be rewarded for his efforts, though, for the tenderness with which he treats his wife in this respect will be returned to him in many loving ways. Nature has provided her with this protection for it is the means by which she develops the habit of saying "no" during those times before marriage that she should. Properly used this aspect of her nature helps to prevent promiscuity.

Are you both aware that a husband is usually sexually aroused rather quickly in the early years of marriage?

This is generally true and will require some adjustment on the part of the wife to accept this part of his nature. He is the aggressor for the family and it shows in this aspect of your marriage. But as he is able to have this release more often he will begin to be able to exercise the control the wife requires. Joining together in solving the problems of this aspect of marriage will help both to have the satisfaction they should be getting from sexual relations.

Sexual Relations

Are you both aware that a wife's attitude toward sexual relations is very much related to her emotional state?

If a wife has some hidden resentment brewing within her she will not respond to sexual relations with her husband in the total-giving kind of passion that both desire. She will withhold a part of herself until that resentment problem has been solved and an astute husband will pick up on this immediately. A wife must *feel* a oneness with her husband before she can give herself to him totally.

The wife must be keenly aware of this part of her nature and share the problem with her husband so that they can both understand its cause. If the husband understands and tries to help, this alone is enough to cause her to respond to him lovingly. Most wives will not demand perfection. Rather they will be able to function freely with just an understanding husband.

Do you tell each other when you are pleased with your sexual relations?

One of the nicest ways to develop openness in discussing sexual matters is to tell your partner when something is especially pleasing. It is a legitimate ego-building device and should be used frequently. Further, if you are pleased with some particular aspect of your sexual relations and you do not tell your partner, you may miss the pleasure of this happening again while waiting in silence hoping for it to happen without your having to say a word.

It might be nice if married couples were clairvoyant and could read minds but they are not. Overcoming the inhibitions each may feel regarding this tender subject is a must. As years grow upon years, couples will become so close that they may seem to be reading each other's minds and emotions.

Do you tell each other when you are not pleased with your sexual relations?

Not telling your partner when something about your sexual relations is unpleasant may cause you to endure needless pain and discomfort that your partner would lovingly change if he or she knew about it. Giving and accepting instructions in this matter should be considered helpful to both of you. The manner in which they are given can build or destroy the ego. Therefore, much care must be exercised in giving critical comment in this regard.

Does either of you feel that you have sexual relations too much or too little?

If so, the first and most important step is to discuss this with your partner. Where there is good will in a marriage an adjustment in attitude will come about by making the desires of one known to the other.

If a wife begins to feel that her husband is using her for sex any time he wants it she will withdraw into a shell and her emotions eventually explode. If a husband is frequently confronted with the "headache" excuse his emotions will start to shatter and may cause him to look elsewhere for the satisfaction he is entitled to from his wife.

Planning special dates for sexual relations with each other may help resolve any problems with regard to too much or too little. This will give you both a chance to anticipate a

Sexual Relations 46

good time instead of having an unplanned encounter that you did not expect.

Are you willing to help each other achieve the kind of satisfaction you want from your sexual relations?

Since it takes two of you to achieve this satisfaction you must give up all inhibitions to talk about it. If you begin to talk with each other on this level to achieve this kind of goal it will help you in other areas of your marriage as well. If either of you is unable to do this then you may be dealing with a level of selfishness that will manifest itself in other areas of your marriage.

Does either of you ever do things to avoid sexual relations with the other?

If you do, you are avoiding another problem about which you refuse to talk with your partner. This is like a cancer on your marriage; you cannot hide it for long. It will grow and kill your marriage unless you discuss this avoidance with each other.

Does either of you ever refuse to have sexual relations with the other?

If you do, you are refusing to solve whatever problem is causing this to happen. A husband and wife are entitled to enjoy this part of marriage with each other and when one refuses this most loving act, something is terribly wrong in the marriage. This kind of behavior can slowly, painfully kill a marriage.

Do you ever resent your partner having a climax in sexual relations when you do not?

It should be the goal of each of you to see to it that the other has this satisfaction from sexual relations. It cannot be one-sided. It is one of the paradoxes of life in that helping the other achieve satisfaction you help yourself as well. Patience is the key for this to happen. If this is a frequent complaint on the part of one, obviously the other partner is being selfish. If it is only an occasional happening but resentment is felt, talk about it, reveal your feelings. No one can win unless you do.

Does either of you show a reluctant attitude about having sexual relations?

If you do, this will take the pleasure that should belong to both away. In no other area of your married life will problems more quickly be revealed than in this most intimate act. Deep down inside, either partner will know why any reluctance is present and if it is not revealed, a martyred attitude may develop that will be harmful to both of you. Think about what is causing your reluctance about something that should be a joy and pleasure to you. Discuss this with your partner.

Does either of you ever feel "used" regarding your sexual relations?

The warmth and love you feel for one another should come to the fore during sexual relations and be expressed in the manner in which you make love. For you to feel "used," love is not being expressed; consent is being given – nothing more. This gets close to lust within marriage. It defeats the purpose of making love and turns into a "taking and getting" rather than a "giving and receiving" act. Your feeling "used" will not change unless your partner is aware of it and you both work on the problem that is causing this feeling to come about.

Does either of you ever use sexual relations as a means of reward or punishment?

Punishments and rewards have no place in the marriage relationship unless, of course, two children are married to each other. Children may be trained in this manner but not a married partner. Marriage assumes a level of maturity that is above this kind of behavior. If either of you is indulging in it, better look inside to see why and then reveal your attitude to your partner.

5

CHILDREN

A man and a woman have been given the power by God to create new life. This power links one generation with the other creating a tree of life called family. Science may explain the manner of his happening; nature may claim it as part of her world; but for most people on the Earth, belief that the power source comes from a Supernatural Being is a creed easily believed when gazing on the beauty of a newborn child.

The power to create new life will usually bring great joy to a husband and wife. The great majority of married couples desire children to be born of their union. In all of recorded history the family, with a mother and father in the home, has been regarded as the ideal environment for the rearing of children.

Before the industrial revolution, an agricultural society existed that depended greatly on the family for support. Children were needed to work and help parents on the farm. Since this revolution, however, a change has occurred in those countries where technology has taken the place of people in the production of agricultural goods.

In the industrialized society, children are a far greater financial charge on couples than in an agricultural one. Parents are expected to feed, house, clothe and educate children until they are at least eighteen years of age, usually with little or no financial help from the children in this endeavor. Therefore, in the industrialized society, children become a greater financial burden on the parents and the inclination to limit the size of the family becomes strong. Parents who want large families must make heroic efforts to support their children.

The need for many hands to help with the work may have changed with technology but the worth of the human being to live has not. In the industrialized society children are not so much desired for their ability to work but rather for the respect for life which their parents share. It is a noble undertaking to become parents.

One of the many benefits of having children is that they will bring a maturing quality to a married couple that can be achieved in no other way. A child must be taught a great deal by its parents but the child will certainly teach as much as he or she is taught. Those who have not experienced the daily care of children do not know the kind of maturity that comes from this kind of care.

When the first child comes into the home it begins to occupy a preponderant amount of time, attention and energy of its parents. But with the demands made comes a corollary: A growth in family love, a broadening, a deepening, an enriching experience that is part of life's never-to-be-ended learning process.

All parents want to make provision for the secure feeling of their children regarding food, clothing, shelter and education. More than these, though, the parents want an atmosphere in which the love flowing back and forth between parent and child will grow. It is in this manner that the child first learns the meaning of love and family life. It is here that the child first begins to be taught how he or she will be expected to act as a parent in the future. The beauty of this learning experience is most magnificent when it is realized that no other family will do it quite like yours.

Children will profoundly affect the relationship between husband and wife. No other aspect of married life will be as strong as that of husband-wife, parent-child. The emotions of both mother and father will soar higher and run deeper when the lives of their children are at stake.

It is in this facet of married life that the feminine and masculine points of view will be quickly asserted. Only when the two views meld into the completeness of one, does the child feel the warmth of his or her parent speaking. Though the child has both mother and father, when the parent speaks the voice should be as one. This cannot happen unless much discussion takes place year after year regarding the ongoing situations that come about as the result of rearing children.

CHILDREN QUESTIONS

Are you physically able to have children?

Many couples discover after marriage that they are unable to conceive a child. The reasons for the inability to do so are numerous and can sometimes be corrected. After a few years of marriage, couples who want children and cannot have them must seek medical advice to see whether or not help is available to them. Wanting their own children is a very natural desire for married couples but if they cannot have their own other options are available for them to experience this most wonderful of gifts from God.

Would you be willing to try to adopt a child or children?

This is a subject that all couples who are contemplating marriage should discuss. What if we can't have children of our own? What will we do? If either the husband or wife wants children ,the other partner is obligated to make his or her view on this subject known. To go through life wanting a child, even if it is not your own blood, and not being able to do so because your spouse does not want an adopted child is a burden too heavy to carry. It will put a strain on the marriage that may not ever be released. That is why it is so important to know your partner's feelings about this subject before the marriage takes place.

Would the physical or mental health of either partner be a factor to be considered in having children?

Children will consume much of the energy, both physical and mental, of their parents. Taking into consideration how much energy each has to give in this regard is a matter of prudence. If physical disability is a part of your marriage you have every right to ask this question and give it serious regard. If mental health is a problem for either spouse it is even more important that the matter of children be discussed.

Are you willing to accept the responsibilities that come with parenthood?

Children change your lives forever. Though they are a joy and blessing to your marriage, your lifestyle will never be the same as it was before the advent of parenthood. Responsibility with a capital R is what every parent faces. Are you ready for it? Will you accept the changes that must be made in your marriage relationship because of your children?

If you become parents without giving much thought to the responsibilities that go with it, you can be in for quite a shock. Marriage requires that you be willing to accept children because, in all probability, you will have them. If you do not want the responsibility and the kind of change in lifestyle this requires, you should not marry at all.

Many couples marry with the intention of "planning" their children only to find that the "plan" didn't work. The "accidental" child is the most frequently conceived one and can bring the greatest joy and happiness to a couple. The "unwanted" child, on the other hand, suffers a pain and torment which is life-long in its effect. No child should ever have this happen to him or her and the parent who does not want the child will suffer great consequences for a lifetime. This is a form of the highest level of immaturity.

Do you believe in controlling conception by use of artificial contraceptives?

This kind of lifestyle means that you will try to prevent the conception of a child during sexual relations because one or both of you do not wish to have a child. There may be many reasons why couples feel this way but it is a form of selfishness to expect the pleasures of marriage without the responsibilities. This is a matter you should discuss seriously.

Artificial contraceptives may be dangerous to your health. They interfere with the natural processes going on in your body and they will certainly affect the emotional health of one or both of you. Their use implies a wish to fulfill sexual pleasure at any time you desire without consequence. But there will always be a consequence. It may seem that contraceptives allow for spontaneity because couples may have intercourse at any time they please without the obligation of having a child. Yet it takes away the very thing sought – spontaneity – at the very moment it is desired most.

Having children demands unselfishness. Desiring sexual relations without the possibility of conceiving a child reveals selfishness. Is this what you want for a married lifestyle?

Do you believe in controlling conception with knowledge about the natural fertility cycle?

The female body has a natural fertile and infertile cycle for conceiving children. The possibility of conception is limited in the female to certain times of the month in which the egg is in a position in her body to be fertilized by the male sperm. Only when this occurs can she conceive a child. This means that there are normally about three weeks of every month in which the female cannot conceive and only a few days when she can conceive. Usually, about five days of the three-week infertile period she will be menstruating and, normally, unable to conceive. This is not always true.

Controlling conception by this method means abstinence from sexual intercourse during the fertile period. While this kind of abstinence may take away some of the desired spontaneity, it does allow for complete spontaneity when sexual intercourse is had during the infertile periods. Further, because abstinence is part of this method, both partners will feel a sense of "loving" more than with artificial means because both make a sacrifice by waiting for the infertile period of the wife.

Women often get a feeling of being "used" when artificial contraceptives are utilized year after year. The wife's health becomes endangered, yet her husband may have sexual satisfaction without regard to endangering his health. If the husband has a vasectomy in order to control conception then his ability to have children is forever barred. No one can see the future and know that they will never want another child. It is a dangerous game to play.

When abstinence periods are exercised by both, neither has to fear for his or her health and they are caring for one another in a most loving way since this means that both are sacrificing for the other.

Romantic interest is another point to be considered with the natural family planning method. Those romantic feelings each had for the other before marriage may get lost if sexual satisfaction can be achieved at any time desire is aroused. If both husband and wife are desirous of sexual relations but must wait for an infertile period of the wife, sexual desire builds day after day for both until sexual fulfillment can be achieved without the possibility of conception. The rhythm of her cycle will cause this to continue month after month.

If both husband and wife use a little imagination they can build up their romantic interest to have a love affair that would be the envy of any romantic novelist. For instance, plan an especially romantic dinner with the wife wearing an appealing negligee and each using his or her imagination to show some intimate, special consideration for the other.

The romance created by the rhythm system can easily make up for any inconvenience or frustration caused by the abstinence period.

Do you believe in abortion to terminate an unwanted pregnancy?

This means doing something to stop the progress of life that has begun through conception. In order for this to happen, it is necessary for the woman to have some type of operation. This may endanger the health of the woman and will, most certainly, kill the life that has begun as an embryo child. Women, in the United States of America, may now legally elect to abort an unborn child without the consent of the father. If you disagree about abortion, great emotional strain will be in store for both of you.

The conception of a child in the womb of a woman makes her vulnerable to the man who impregnated her to a degree that is not found in any other relationship. The father must take on the responsibility he has created by promising to provide a home and protection for the mother and child. The mother needs this protection in order to fulfill her responsibility of nurturing the child. When these ingredients are missing and a child has been conceived, all kinds of chaos develop in the relationship and in the society in which they live.

No mother wants to hurt her own child unless she is psychotic. Abortion is the ultimate hurt. It brings on psychological problems to the couple and the community that are serious and difficult to control. The sense of loss a woman must endure when her child is pulled from her womb cannot be endured without psychological scars. Even the most jaded of persons cannot endure this loss without feeling it deeply. Society cannot regulate these feelings. It may give permission but it cannot give freedom from guilt.

It is especially important for a man to know how a woman feels about abortion. She has the legal control over the life of their child. It is also important for a woman to know how a man feels about abortion. She will not want to be in the position of having conceived a child and then be asked to abort it because he does not want the responsibility of a child.

What is of the utmost importance in this question is that both the man and woman realize the consequences of sexual union. The time to prevent abortion is before consenting to sexual union.

The other aspect to abortion that should be considered is the presence of selfishness in the relationship. Abortion is an act of selfishness because one or both of the parties are seeking to escape the responsibility that goes along with sexual union – the conception of a child. Selfishness can kill a relationship as well as a child in the womb.

Does either of you believe in vasectomy for men or tubal ligation for women?

Vasectomy for men involves the surgical removal of the convoluted duct that conveys sperm from the testicle to the ejaculatory duct of the penis. It prevents the man from being able to cause conception to occur in that his sperm will never be able to fertilize the ovum, or egg, of the woman.

Tubal ligation for women involves surgical closing of the Fallopian tubes that carry the ova, or eggs, from the ovaries to the uterus. It prevents a woman from being able to conceive in that her eggs will never be in a position in her body to be fertilized.

Both of these operations are for the purpose of being able to have sexual union at any time it is desired without the possibility of conception of a child. They should be considered irrevocable for life.

This type of operation means that a man and woman or husband and wife want to enjoy the benefits of sexual union but do not wish to incur the responsibilities of parenting if conception should occur. Further, it does away with the necessity of using artificial or natural contraceptive measures.

Consideration should be given as to whether this type of thinking will be carried over into other areas of life as well. In all probability it will. For instance, does one wish to enjoy the benefits of having a wife, or husband, but not the responsibility of being married?

A decision regarding either of these operations is very important to the relationship and should be discussed thoroughly with your partner. It involves relinquishing your power to create those who will inherit the next generation to others who do not relinquish it. If you take this drastic step, will you change your mind about having children after a few years of marriage?

Does either of you have a religious belief that would affect your judgment in the matter of birth control?

Many people of various religious faiths believe that life is sacred and the possibility of conception of children is a sacred part of sexual union between a husband and wife. They believe it is what gives this act its loving power.

Some people may wish to limit the number of children to whom they are willing, or able, to give their love and attention. Religious belief may play an important role in the manner in which this limitation occurs. If you, as a couple, want to limit the number of children you have, you should consult with your religious leader about the manner in which you do this.

Your enlightened conscience is the final authority in this matter, but you must enlighten your conscience before a decision so serious can be made.

Do you have definite ideas about the education of children?

During the pre-school years in the life of your child or children, you are the primary educators. You will be the dominant influence in your child's life and he/she will learn from you. Once your child reaches the age for schooling, however, the education of your child will be taken over by others. The school will become a new and powerful influence in your life and that of your child. Each weekday will begin with the preparation of your child for the teacher and school that you have chosen. When your child arrives home from school, more time and consideration will be given to education and therefore the education of your child will begin to control your life to a great extent.

Few parents are able, financially, to exercise the kind of control they would like to have over the education of their children due to the taxing power of the government and its insistence that only public schools will receive tax money. Therefore, public schools may be your only choice if you are not wealthy. Nevertheless, this subject should be discussed with each other so that you know the thinking of your partner.

Do you want a religious education for your children?

Some religious faiths provide full-time schooling for children of their faith. Oftentimes these schools are not so expensive as to be prohibitive to parents who will make some sacrifice for the education offered. Parents should remember, though, that true religious education should come from them.

Some churches provide weekly religious education classes for children in public schools. This may be another way for your child to receive religious instruction in the faith of your choice. These classes are advantageous for the teaching of moral values to children in a group setting. Most parents will consider this necessary for the proper growth of their children.

Would you consider putting a pre-school age child in a nursery?

This is usually done for one reason only. The mother either wants or needs to return to work for financial reasons. Much discussion about this should take place.

If you decide to do put your child in a day care center your infant will be placed in a situation that is not a normal one. It will also cause strain and stress for the mother since it is she who would normally provide the care for this child in its formative years. You should discuss the fact that the child will bond with, and give affection to, whoever is caring for it. Therefore, the mother may be disappointed that she is not receiving the love and affection from the child that would normally be hers.

Pertinent questions should be asked and answered. Is the additional money really needed? Will the net amount of money the mother brings in be worth the sacrifices that will be made by the entire family? Does the mother want this solution as a means of getting out of the house or away from the children?

There is no substitute for the valuable service mothers give to the rearing of their infant children. Therefore, every alternative should be investigated before making this drastic decision.

Do you want pre-kindergarten education for your children?

An only child, or one that is divided by several years from younger or older children in the home, may benefit greatly from the few hours of being with other children the same age. It may benefit the mother too to have a few hours free from caring for the child for a few days each week.

Parents should investigate thoroughly the type of atmosphere their young child will be in when they consider pre-kindergarten schooling. If the staff of teachers is a good one the child may learn quickly in the group setting with other children.

Do you want your children to have a college education?

This may seem a foolish question since most every parent will answer yes. However, parents need to remember that when the time comes for this decision to be made it will be your child who makes it. Parents can only help to make a college education available to their child. Pressuring a child to attend college when he or she does not want to go seldom ends in success.

It may be surprising to you as a couple to find out how different your views are on a college education for your children. This kind of endeavor will seriously affect your lives and should be fully discussed so that you know each other's thinking on this subject.

Would you borrow money for the education of your children?

This subject is one for serious discussion. If you agree that you are willing to do this it will probably be the largest expenditure you make during your marriage. A college education often costs more than a home and certainly more than a car. If you are in agreement about this matter, then you can probably accomplish this goal, but if you are not, it can cause serious trouble in your marriage.

6

PERSONAL CHARACTER

Personal character is formed by the judgment we use in accepting or rejecting those ideas to which we are exposed. They become the values we choose and form the basis of our lifestyle. The values each brings to their marriage relationship form its shape, determine its destiny and reveal its possibilities.

How do you discover what these ideas are that play so important a role in your married life and all those who will be affected by it? Only by probing the mind, feeling the emotions and looking into the soul of another, can each person really know the partner they want to marry.

But before this happens, the foremost person to investigate is one's self. The age-old admonition to "know thyself" takes on large significance when trying to blend your life with another in marriage because it is here that your character will be expressed in its rawest form. The "person" you are deep inside will be exposed and your virtues and vices will be revealed unquestionably. It is part of the human condition that all have these. Daily life in marriage is a matter of discovering what they are – not whether they exist.

Your character will first be revealed by the honor and regard in which you hold others with whom you conduct your life. Honor is the virtue that shows respect, gives dignity and conveys esteem on all those for whom regard should be held. If you place a high value on this virtue, no deed causing shame, scandal or loss of regard will be engaged in that will bring loss of esteem to yourself and others.

Those who hold themselves in good regard rarely treat others differently. We tend to reveal what we think of ourselves by how we treat others close in our lives. It is our nature to think well of our own self. If we do not, something is wrong. In the daily contact of marriage each partner will most likely treat the other very much according to what each thinks of him or herself. In other words, if you have little regard for yourself, your partner will likely be treated poorly. On the other hand, if you hold yourself in good regard, your partner will likely be treated with respect.

Discovering the character you have formed usually cannot be done until the transition from adolescence to adulthood has been completed. Hopefully, the formation of character has taken place before the advent of marriage. But how can you be sure this has happened? It is obvious to see that the body has grown but it is not so obvious to see the growth of the mind, the emotions and the spirit.

One way of determining whether or not good character has been formed is whether or not you are able to "support" yourself. The word "support" may mean many things used in this context. Some of the ways of judging this is if you are earning your own livelihood. Are you responsible for the purchase and care of your clothing? Can you properly prepare a meal for yourself and clean your own living quarters without aid? Are you able to pay for your own shelter whether you are living at home or with parents? If all of these are true then you are able to "support" yourself. You have become independent of others.

As a result of this independence the natural adjustments in a marriage relationship will be easier for you than for those who did not assume these responsibilities. If you did not take on the quest for personal independence then you will probably bring a child-like atmosphere of being cared for into your marriage relationship. If your marriage is to succeed the natural selfishness of a child must undergo the transition into a responsible, giving adult.

In marriage, the more responsibility each partner assumes, the less chance one partner will become the "parent" of the other and thereby prevent the transition to independence from taking place. In a marriage where two wish to become one with the other, each is giving freely, totally, to the other without a word being said about it.

No vocation in life allows you to attain as much happiness and independence as does marriage. Within the boundaries of the laws of God and nature and man-made laws and codes of ethics you are free to live a life of sheer ecstasy in communion with another human being you have vowed to love. Most couples will want to rely on those unfailing *truths* revealed through the centuries and handed down from generation to generation. In designing your marriage you may want to deny or ignore these but they will not go away. Their consequences will eventually have to be dealt with. These *truths* form the boundaries from which you cannot stray without paying the price. But within these boundaries you have great freedom to mold a life style strictly your own. Your character traits will profoundly influence and determine the kind of marriage you will be able to build.

The foundation stones of building a good marriage will sound like a list of virtues in a book: trustworthy, patient, considerate, polite, prompt. These are not mere words to a married couple. Rather, these words come alive and touch the emotions every day. Simply being kind to one another every hour of every day is probably the most valuable asset to any marriage.

Revealing your innermost self is the delicate but welcome task each married couple should perform. In order to do this, many subjects, common to both, should be talked about endlessly. As you do this you will find that a unique quality is being developed in your marriage that is special to just the two of you. This quality is what gives your marriage its beauty, its elegance, its grace, its symmetry. When married couples do not reveal themselves to one another in this special way, their marriage will reveal its ugliness, its stumbling, its lack of design. A drab picture will begin to form and ultimately the marriage may fail.

You marry because you love someone. But the personal virtues and vices and the character you have formed will determine the *quality of love* you will share with each other. By "knowing yourself" you can build on those virtues you have and control those vices that weaken you. The Creator has endowed each of us with a free will to act in our own behalf for our own good. Use your free will to make your marriage the best it can be.

Personal Character

The Creator has complemented the whole male person with the whole female person. This brings forth a grace to each that was not there before. Henceforth you can act in unison for the good of both. When you have formed your personal character into a *moral and mature person* you are now able to become one with the other.

Henceforth you can act in unison for the good of both. You are now able to know one another in depth and help each other grow in the maturity of life. Your love for one another should make this task the delight of your lives. It is the reason you chose to live together in the first place.

PERSONAL CHARACTER QUESTIONS

Are you trustworthy?

In a marriage relationship you must be able to rely on each other for truth and honesty. It is the cornerstone of any marriage. Always being able to rely on your partner to tell the truth is a right you should be able to expect. The beauty of being able to trust your partner, no matter what situation, will build a bond between you that no one can break. Married people who are trustworthy to one another, from the beginning of their days to the end, bring a joy and contentment to their lives that is beautiful and peaceful to behold.

Marriage is the uniting of two people who hope to meld their lives into one. If you are unable to trust your married partner, the whole flavor and meaning of marriage changes. It becomes degrading and humiliating when trust is broken.

Thereafter, doubt and suspicion are your constant companions. Your spirits will never be able to soar as one.

Are you patient?

Patience is a gift that two people in love can give to one another. It is a rare quality that separates a marriage from the ordinary to the sublime. It means having the ability to wait or endure without complaint. Oftentimes husbands and wives must bear with one another's pace in order not to run ahead, thereby losing the other. It means putting up with idiosyncrasies in your partner that you may find peculiar. We all have them and your partner will be experiencing the same irritation you do. If you don't believe offering this gift to your beloved in marriage, and receiving it in return, is sublime, then watch a married couple who do not offer it in their dealings with one another. You will hardly be able to believe that they truly love one another.

Impatience implies seeking one's own way, regardless of the result to the partner. This attitude can be disastrous to the marriage relationship. The difficulty with exercising patience is that it must be called forth every moment of every day. Human weakness makes this a near impossibility but a sufficient quantity of patience shown to your spouse brings unexpected rewards never anticipated, and enchanting when they are received.

Are you considerate?

Consideration in marriage means being treated in a courteous and polite manner at all times. If you say "please" and "thank you" to your friends and business associates, how much more the need to say these small words of appreciation to your spouse. Your spouse's service to you is far greater than any service you will receive from another person.

Just because you are married does not mean a relaxation of the rules of courtesy. Being inconsiderate or impolite indicates a lack of the kind of love that should be present in the marriage relationship. Politeness to one another in marriage is an outward manifestation of an inward belief that you married a lady or gentleman. You did, didn't you?

Are you prompt?

Promptness means being ready without delay. In a marriage it sets the tone of your day from the moment you awake. It means being prompt about getting up and going to work on time. About doing your daily household chores. About fixing meals for the family at the proper time. About paying your bills on time. About going to bed at a reasonable hour. Many good times can be enjoyed in private, in business and in social engagements when promptness is exercised the way it should be.

When you habitually fail to be prompt in your daily life, you become difficult and unpleasant to live with. Further, you become known as an unreliable person. If you are habitually late for activities planned with another person, then you spoil their good time to the point where they would rather not include you in these times in the future. When you are married and you are habitually late in all you do, you put your partner in an impossible position. Your marriage partner is not free to exclude you as all other persons are.

Are you able to love other people in spite of their faults and limitations?

Everyone has imperfections in their personality and character. Each of us has limitations on our abilities of mind and emotions. As you grow and mature you will readily see these faults and limitations in your family, friends, and business acquaintances. Yet, each of us wants to be liked and loved for who we are and not who someone else wants us to be. Learning to love and accept others with their imperfections is part of being an adult. All of this is magnified in a marriage. The close living that the marriage relationship requires means that each partner must be tolerant of any imperfections in their partner that at times seem to irritate. Every husband and wife wants and needs to be loved in this way.

Do you have a cheerful disposition? Do you have a sense of humor?

A pleasant disposition is one of the most valuable traits in any person. In a marriage partner it is a treasure. Being able to laugh at our foibles, at our mistakes, makes us attractive to be around. This characteristic has been given to human beings alone. A cheerful disposition and a sense of humor can carry a married couple through many hard times. It keeps priorities straight and makes troubles seem light or even disappear.

All of us have experienced life with a family member, a teacher or a friend who habitually displayed a "sour" disposition and countenance. None of us imagine that this person would be pleasant to live with. Sometimes we are forced to accept such a person in our company for a short period of time but we are always anxious to get away from them as soon as possible. In a marriage relationship this kind of person will spoil it everyday of life. Even a loving spouse will grow weary and tired of having to deal with this kind of personality for the rest of his or her life. It will ruin your marriage relationship. It may be embarrassing to do so, but it is not out of bounds for married partners to discuss this with one another.

Have you learned to share what you have with others?

Sharing is a lesson learned with great difficulty. Ask any parent who has to settle the squabbles of children over sharing their belongings. Brothers and sisters often fight endlessly about their "personal" possessions (usually given to them by another person). They are young and immature and we tend to forgive their behavior while trying to teach them the value of sharing. It is a lesson that must be learned if success as an adult is to be hoped for. Your adult life is not fully developed until you are able to share your life with others and realize that by doing so you are taking the only path to true personal happiness.

In a marriage, sharing is an absolute necessity. If your marriage partner has not learned this lesson, he or she will hold back on time, energy, money, praise, thankfulness, cooperation, even love. This lack of maturity makes married life miserable.

UNDESIRABLE CHARACTER TRAITS

There are some undesirable character traits that will be an impediment to becoming one in a marriage relationship. They are vices that destroy those virtues necessary for this to happen. You should want to know if any of these are impeding your progress to becoming one with your beloved.

Do you seek undue advantage in your dealings with people?

Fairness is at stake here. Inwardly everyone knows whether or not they are fair to others or seek undue advantage of them. Outwardly those who deal with you will know this too, by judging the manner in which you deal with them.

Of all the people on earth that you should be fair with it is your marriage partner. Because of the intimacy involved, each of you knows well whether or not you are fair with each other or takes advantage of your partner's kind nature. If you constantly vie and contend with each other over most aspects of your married life then one or both is seeking undue advantage over the other.

Do you have an unreasonable temper?

This is probably one of the most difficult vices to deal with in a marriage relationship. If an unreasonable temper is present in your personality, then your partner in marriage never knows at what moment your violent temper will explode. This causes endless anxiety that begins to affect your partner's personality. Reason cannot be used to control such a temper – it has to die of its own exhaustion. These are the warning signs: Inability to argue out an issue; a difference of opinion resolved by walking out; a hand raised against you in order to win a point. Only a foolish heart continues to live with an unwillingness to change an unreasonable temper. Your partner's professed love is a lie unless he or she is willing to seek help in growing to a mature level that does not include an unreasonable temper.

Are you envious of others?

Envy means discontentment and can never be satisfied. It can ruin the good feeling of accomplishments and rob you of the precious satisfaction that should be yours for those things done according to your ability – not another's. The wife who constantly complains of her husband's efforts to provide for her chips away at his self-confidence every day of his life. Even if he tries to meet her demands his heart and mind will turn away from her. The husband who can never be satisfied is equally destructive.

A marriage relationship unequivocally demands that husband and wife encourage one another's talents and efforts – not belittle them. Envy is not to be mistaken for ambition, though. A strong desire to succeed or achieve is necessary to life.

Are you unreasonably jealous?

Jealousy is virtuous in its reasonable application, i.e., being jealous of one's rights; guarding that which belongs to you from another. But unfounded jealousy in a marriage is destructive in its lack of trust. Trustworthiness in marriage implies doing nothing that would cause one's partner to fear for his or her rights.

Once you take each other in marriage, no look, gesture, word or deed should arise involving others that would cause concern or worry to your spouse. This is a right of marriage and should be jealously guarded. To imagine these things occurring, to be constantly looking for them without foundation, is unreasonable. Jealousy then becomes a vice. Between couples of good will, discussion can dispel doubts and love made the stronger for it.

Are you conceited?

Conceit is a particularly difficult vice to live with in another person. It can be a time-consuming partner on a daily basis. It is a form of selfishness that someone must serve and, in a marriage, one's partner is usually the servant. It means being subject to your partner's exaggerated opinion of self.

Inward conceit manifests itself outwardly in the form of over-preoccupation with actions and appearance. If one is constantly concerned about looks and behavior, it will be difficult to intrude on this love affair with self. To concentrate on being neatly and attractively dressed, then forgetting yourself in order to pay attention to other people, brings a genuineness that is lacking in the selfishness of conceit. Recognizing that the problem of conceit exists may be difficult but it is the first step to change. Married partners can be of immense help to one another in this endeavor if true charity is exercised. Criticism should not carry a hurtful sting.

Do you habitually tell dirty jokes and stories when in business or social groups?

Dirty jokes do seem to please many in the crowd when you are in public. Some show people believe they must include some of these in their repertoire in order to please everyone. But some in the crowd will be offended even in this situation.

In private social gatherings the case is usually different. In this setting the off-color stories may be only tolerated. If they are too offensive, guests may not be asked to socialize again. There is a fine line between the funny and the offensive in this game of jokes and stories. If you cannot walk this line you should not play the game lest you fall on the wrong side.

If your married partner objects to your behavior regarding these jokes and stories, out of consideration for your spouse you should curtail the telling of these stories.

Do you swear or use vulgar language habitually?

Swearing or using vulgar language in your daily speech habits usually produces a lack of respect for you by your colleagues. They may consider this a lack of education on your part because your vocabulary is so limited.

As a youth the use of vulgar language and swearing are often resorted to in efforts to impress peers and to be "one of the crowd." But as adolescents grow into adults this habit should be quickly changed and forgotten. Few adults really admire a person who habitually flavors his or her language with swearing and vulgarity. Most adults try to avoid this type of person as much as possible. It is a sure sign of immaturity.

To expect that your partner in marriage will enjoy listening to daily swearing or vulgarity is ignorance in the sublime. It will be a matter of shame and embarrassment to your spouse whether you are in private or in a group of people.

It is a habit rather easily broken by concentration on it and your partner will probably be most happy to help you rid yourself of this objectionable habit.

What is your attitude regarding nudity in public?

One of the most precious gifts of marriage is the physical giving of one to the other and to no other person. Reverencing the body in the sanctity of marriage prohibits the public display of it in any way disrespectful to your spouse. Nudity is a precious part of your private life and each of you will cherish the tender moments alone with each other this way. It is not a spectator sport. Many people resent the crudeness of nudity outside the bedroom scene.

Many forms of nudity are in vogue today and partial nudity is run of the mill for television shows even in daytime and early evening. This is a form of brainwashing to make it seem like this is an acceptable form of behavior and many people succumb to this type of thinking. Books, movies, television, stage shows, concerts and social gatherings abound with various forms of nudity in an attempt to obtain social acceptance.

In marriage, if this type of thinking becomes your behavior, then it will spell disaster to your relationship. If you dress immodestly or succumb to total nakedness with others viewing your body, your spouse cannot help but be offended. If he or she is not, then something is missing from your marriage relationship. Your spouse's body may not belong to you but it has been promised and given to you in marriage and to no other. If it is flaunted in front of others, there cannot help but be a feeling of loss.

7

FAMILY AND HERITAGE

Of all the influences affecting marriage the family is probably the strongest. Yet this aspect of marriage has gone through the greatest changes in recent decades. In times past, parents arranged the marriage and the couple somehow learned to love one another after the ceremony was over. The musical *Fiddler On The Roof*, marvelously portrays this practice and the difficulties inherent in it. *Romeo and Juliet* is a sad drama of the consequences that can result from such customs.

Nowadays, however, people meet, are drawn to each other, and sometimes marry without the parents knowing about it. Television and movies abound with stories of such happenings and wars catapulted this custom into a commonplace occurrence. Both of these extremes have advantages and disadvantages.

Regardless of the manner in which you got married, no other aspect will more deeply affect your lives than will your relationship with your two families. Normally, no one is ever as close to you as your parents until you meet the person you fall in love with. As a result of this close parental association your married lives should be enriched by a new relationship with both sets of parents. But it is not a relationship that is always easy to achieve. Different beliefs and customs have to be accommodated in order for this to happen.

In the course of living your married life you will often wish to have some guidance from a trusted person. Seldom will you be able to find persons who would combine the qualities of good judgment and trust more than parents. You should be able to benefit from their experience in life and few people will voice ideas to you with as little self-interest and as much your-interest as parents. Even if they have not been able to take their own good advice parents will usually give their best wisdom to their children hoping they will be able to accept it.

Living parents provide your children with one of the most endearing relationships known – grandparent to grandchild. There is no other source for your children to know this kind of love.

If your family includes brothers and sisters then unity of family life can be sweet and beautiful in all respects. You will be able to rely on the experience that only time has given your parents and you can have the feeling of warmth that the growing years brought to brotherly and sisterly relationships. Brothers and sisters can give you the sympathetic understanding of contemporaries in your own generation that parents cannot give and this understanding will be unlike any you can get from your friends. Also, your children will be blessed with aunts and uncles who will love them as no others.

The manner of life you lived with your parents formed the basis of your ideas regarding marriage. Their home was the only school available on this subject. It is hoped that it was a happy home because the greatest gift parents can give, outside of life, is their own personal happiness and contentment with each other in their married life.

If your parents resented the restrictions that being married places on everyone, then they could not convey a sense of happiness and contentment to you. If they did not willingly make the sacrifices essential to the rearing of children, then this will have been an impediment to your sense of security and your feeling loved as a child. All kinds of doubts about marriage will have entered your mind.

When you marry, this family from which you grew must now be blended with that of another family, your partner's. Frequently, those about to be married staunchly proclaim that they are not marrying the family but, rather, each other. After the marriage, however, they discover that though they were not marrying the family, they have married *into* it. Acceptance by members of the family of each spouse becomes significantly important to both.

The family that becomes your "family-in-law" is not "in love" with you and may not accept your personality as easily as your spouse did. Therefore, your acceptance may depend on your words and actions toward them. If they voiced objections to your marriage those should be given attention. They may contain a truth that you have overlooked or are glossing over. If the objections were real, they will not disappear. If they were not, then your parents-in-law will discover this and want the success of your marriage. They will be anxious for the objections they voiced to cease to exist. Parents will never want to be shut out from the lives of their adult children.

Another aspect of family life that may affect your marriage relationship is the cultural heritage in both of your backgrounds. In this day and age this may seem unimportant, yet, ethnic background and its culture will cause certain characteristics to be brought to your marriage relationship that are indelible and which will have an effect on your lives daily. Special consideration for this fact, not only for yourselves but for your families, needs to be dominant in your minds in order for the necessary adjustments to be made that will ensure a good relationship with your spouse's family.

Cultural heritage may result in a desire for special kinds of food for one or both of you. Certain customs that have no meaning for one may be critically significant to the other. More important, cultural heritage may cause your partner to expect a certain role from you as husband or wife that is peculiar to his or her ethnic background. These are not insurmountable obstacles to marital happiness but they do demand considerable discussion, deep respect and understanding between you.

In the assimilation process of one culture into another in this country, people are sometimes made to feel inferior or be degraded because of their ethnic background. When this happens, whether real or imagined, a person may try to turn away from their heritage because it caused such personal hurt. For instance, if the name is peculiar to their national background and is difficult for others to pronounce, it may be changed. Personal, social, and even business reasons may make this seem wise. If the hurt was deep enough, the person may not want his or her children associated in any way with the feelings of disapproval he or she felt and turn away from his or her own ancestors.

As time passes, however, both the assimilation process and the wisdom of years will usually soften this attitude and an appreciation for the cultural heritage may be renewed. It may even become more fervent as appreciation sometimes is accompanied by a sense of guilt for having turned away in the first place. Ethnic prejudice can be acute in youth, but age usually causes people to realize that all cultures and races have these differences and each, in its own way, serves human beings with similar needs, hopes and desires.

Most people are able to function very well in a bi-cultural atmosphere. In a marriage it is essential when two cultures are brought together in one family. If one partner is unable to do it, the marriage will suffer as well as the family relationship.

If your marriage has brought together two cultures, you need to discover the differences and similarities in your backgrounds and know the implications these bring to your relationship with one another. While it presents certain problems, it also provides the spice of variety that others may lack in their lives.

You are now two with the hope of becoming one in a marriage. Your families will play an important role in your ability to make this happen. Ask questions and meet your spouse's family before you marry so that you will know the role expected of you from this group of people. It is true that you have not married *them* but never forget that you have married *into* their way of life.

FAMILY AND HERITAGE QUESTIONS

Do you know the place of birth and citizenship of your partner?

This may seem like such a basic question that it is ridiculous to ask. Yet it is surprising how many couples have only vague ideas about the answer. The place of birth of your spouse was one in which, normally, he or she grew up. Different customs and cultures are associated with different parts of the country. A Californian is not a New Yorker. There is a big difference. If you do not ask this question, then how do you know if your partner came from another country? If he or she did, you need to know whether or not your partner became a citizen. Do not assume the answer to this question.

Do you know the manner in which your partner spent his or her youth?

It is normal to be raised by one's natural parents, among one's relatives in the country of one's birth. This is not always the case and many people are raised in other circumstances. This will have had an effect on his or her life. If there are any unusual circumstances regarding the manner in which you were raised, your married partner cannot fully understand you as a person unless he or she knows this. Talk about it.

Do you love and respect your parents?

Life is a precious gift that must be nurtured with many years of love and care to be sustained. It is because you received this gift from your parents that they deserve your love and respect. You will want this from your children too.

Sometimes parents are not good ones and their grown children have a right to resent what happened to them in their youth. If it was severe enough it may be the cause for alienation in adulthood. However, you cannot get away from the fact that they gave you life. Try to respect that much at least.

Are your parents proud of you?

Loving obedience in the home is the reward children constantly give parents for sacrifices made for them. If you were obedient to your parents, deferred to their judgment instead of your own while you were a youth, then they will be proud of you. This is really what all loving parents want from their children.

If there is any reason why your parents are not proud of you, your spouse has a right to know this fact. He or she will have to deal with the deprivation of the enrichment that this family should provide in your married life. If you are sufficiently justified in your reason, then your partner will understand and make allowances for the loss this entails. If you are not, then your partner may be of help in closing the breach between you and your parents for the benefit of both you, and your children.

Did you argue with your parents a great deal through your adolescent years?

If you did there were ideas that they had regarding life standards and values that you did not wish to accept or adopt as your own. You would not defer to their judgment until adulthood. Some deep thought will be necessary on your part to determine the correct course for you to follow. If your differences were great enough they may be a divisive factor the rest of your life. If they were not, then some accommodation may be possible that will allow a compatible relationship in adulthood.

Do you have a close relationship with your parents?

It is hoped that you do. Most couples want one. The closeness you feel with your parents after marriage will depend in great measure on your partner's ability to allow this. Each partner will ordinarily appreciate any kindness and consideration shown to their parents. On the other hand, any unkindness will usually be resented and may have an effect on your marriage relationship. This will especially be true on the death of the parents. In all probability they will die before either of you and the loss of their presence in your lives will be deeply felt.

Do you like being in the company of each of your parents?

This can be a sensitive subject to discuss but all couples need to do it. If you gave careful consideration to the feelings of these two families before you married, you can establish a warm and friendly relationship rather quickly. If you did not, you will have to build one from strained feelings. It is a question that cannot be ignored because to do nothing is to do something. Your parents will visit your home and you will visit theirs in all probability. It puts a strain on your marriage if you do not like these people and do not enjoy the time spent with them.

Do you call each other's parents "Mom" and "Dad" or some similar tern to express their special relationship to you?

The answer to this question reveals much about your inner feelings regarding these two people. It is an indication of the kind of relationship you want. You may feel uncomfortable calling a woman "Mom" who is not your mother and a man "Dad" who is not your father. This feeling should be honored and it is acceptable to call these people by their first names instead. There is no disrespect shown when this happens and neither of you should resent the other feeling this way about their parents.

Is there a feeling of unity in the lives of both families?

If so, you can establish a life style with them. If not, you may need to build relationships similar to these with close friends. Sometimes this is a very satisfactory alternative as you can pick those you want in your inner circle. If closeness is felt on one side of the family and not on the other, tension can develop. It can only be relieved by much discussion between married partners.

Does either of you feel you spend too much time with either of your parents?

Leaving the parental home is often difficult both physically and emotionally. Yet your time now belongs to each other first – family second. You must help each other grow away from parents and toward one another. This will not be hard if there is good will from both of you. If your spouse thinks you spend too much time with your parents, you had better pay attention to this complaint and deal with it.

Does either of you feel that the other relies too much on the judgment of parents and not enough on one another?

Learning to depend on one another is part of your job as a married couple. It helps you grow and mature as individuals and as a couple. Parental advice may be sought but, in the last analysis, you, as a couple, must make decisions that will affect your lives.

Does either of you feel that your mothers interfere too much in your lives?

The mothers of both partners can supply much needed love, affection and, on occasion, help, that no other person will be able to duplicate. However, this "help" should not go so far as to become interference in your lives and how you want to live. If either of you feels that one of your mothers is spending too much time in your home or interfering in your lives, then you need to talk about it. Pay very close attention to your spouse's objections because it is your partner who is entitled to your time and attention – not your mother. After you have come to a conclusion, it should be the son or daughter of the mother who should speak to her about this matter.

Do your parents have objectionable habits that you do not want to have in your marriage relationship?

If so, you must pay particular attention to these in order to avoid them. You must concentrate on the particular habits you want to change because it will be your natural inclination to imitate your parents and their life style.

Does either of you ever help members of your family when the other feels neglected?

If the answer is yes, then you have trouble saying "no" to a member of your family when it is necessary or advisable. The happiness of your married partner comes first. Talk about the problem with your spouse and try to come to a mutual understanding before insisting on helping family first. Sometimes your partner will be able to be more objective in this situation than you are.

Does either of you insist that the other put up with members of your family when one partner specifically does not want to?

This can be a most difficult problem if there is strong family feeling involved. Your married partner deserves first consideration always. If this is a problem in your marriage your partner will have reasons for feeling the way he or she does. You need to explore these reasons and determine if they are reasonable ones. If love exists, tolerance will be exercised.

Does either of you ever allow a member of your family to ridicule the other in your presence?

If this kind of conversation takes place it is a very serious matter that will breed feelings of contempt toward the marriage partner if allowed to continue. You chose to marry your spouse because you loved him or her. Allowing anyone, particularly family, to ridicule this person in front of you is an insult to the decision you made and to your partner. You must take action so that your family members will know that you will not tolerate it.

Do you discuss any problems about your parents with each other first, then allow the son or daughter to handle it with his or her parents?

A son or daughter will be able to talk in an intimate way with parents that the in-law may not be able to do. In most cases, parents too would feel freer to discuss openly any problems they may have with their own child.

Have your cultural backgrounds given you strong preferences for certain kinds of foods?

If so, the problems you will face may be easily glossed over in the dating stage but become very serious after marriage when daily life must be lived. Adapting your tastes to foods from one culture to another is not usually difficult but will take some accommodating. Learning to cook new recipes may be fun and interesting but it can also be irritating sometimes.

Holiday dinners with families from different backgrounds may also present problems you will have to solve. The customs associated with certain cultures have been handed down through the generations and usually have a beautiful meaning connected to the ritual of celebrating them. Learning the meaning of these customs and trying to include them in your family life is an act of love your partner cannot help but appreciate. If you are in a bi-cultural marriage, learning to appreciate the ethnic differences you live with is a must.

Family and Heritage

Have your cultural backgrounds caused you to expect a particular role to be played by husbands and wives?

If so, your partner has a right to agree or disagree to play this "expected" role. This type of unconscious expectation is very subtle in its effect. If you find yourself caught in this situation, you have a right and obligation to insist on talking this out thoroughly and designing your own marriage role within legitimate boundaries.

Will you want your children to speak a language related to your cultural background?

An ability to speak more than one language should be considered an asset at all times. Yet, feelings can be intense about this subject in a bi-cultural marriage. First consideration should be given to the language spoken in America, English. A second language is desirable but children need to know the language that will be used by others when they reach adulthood and seek a job.

Does your cultural background have certain aspects to it that you do not want to impart to your children?

If there are certain aspects regarding your cultural heritage that have caused you embarrassment or humiliation you may shun away from having your children experience this kind of hurt. If your background has been a deterrent to your ability to progress in your career choice, you may become more alienated and try to keep your children from this kind of treatment.

The emotional reactions you have to these situations should be thoroughly discussed with your partner so that you can act in unison in resolving whatever difficulties you face.

Have you changed your name to alter the ethnic connotation your real name may carry?

Many people do this for purposes of shortening their name for business reasons or changing it so that the name alone will not immediately associate them with a particular nationality group. If you have done this, certainly your partner in marriage needs this information and your reasons for doing it.

Most people are proud of their heritage and would never consider changing their name. This is admirable and should be encouraged.

8

RELIGION

The subject of religion is of paramount importance to two people contemplating marriage. It is from religion that our moral foundation is formed. We get this from no other place.

Religious faith is a beautiful and wonderful asset to any marriage. Two people who acknowledge their Creator as an authority outside of themselves for their personal behavior have a much better chance of succeeding in a marriage relationship.

If you have not personally confronted whether or not you believe in God by the time of marriage, you should do so. No one goes through life without answering the question, "Is there a God?" You may not do it consciously but everyone, by his or her actions, will answer this question.

A crisis of religious faith often takes place at about the same time marriage is contemplated. If you have experienced a desire for an understanding of the religious faith in which you were raised, this is normal. Most persons want to gain some knowledge about other religious faiths at this time in order to make a decision for themselves about which religious faith they choose to belong. By the time of marriage, though, there should be a decision about the religious faith you want to share between you and in which to raise your children.

In your marriage, religious beliefs and doctrines will have a stabilizing influence in your dealings with each other and provide the necessary guidance for both of you in all aspects of your married life. For this reason your religious faith can be the most valued asset in your marriage relationship.

If you have divergent views about religion it is imperative that you discuss these thoroughly. In this case you will have to make adjustments that will allow for your different beliefs to be accommodated. This should always be done in an amicable way. Religion is not a subject to argue about but it is one to discuss. If you do no discuss this subject with each other then you run the risk of having difficulties come between you that destroy the peace and ease that should be present in your home.

Divergent religious outlooks may be an impediment to the two of you becoming one. These differences in beliefs can grow and deprive you of an important measure of quiet and ease that other good marriages develop. On the other hand, many couples are very successful at holding different views about religion.

No one should presume to intrude on your inalienable right to worship God as you please, even your partner in marriage. The hurt of such an intrusion can have a disastrous effect. Discussion of this subject should be conducted with gentleness and consideration. The discussion of this subject and the decisions you make regarding it will be a central focus in all of your years together.

The reward for sincere religious faith is peace of mind and soul on earth and eternal life after death. With this much at stake, it is essential that you help each other grow in your religious faith and thereby mature in your spiritual lives.

Your religious beliefs will have a formative impact on your children since you will impart your views to them in their young and adolescent years. They need this influence in their lives and it is most important that it comes from you as their parents. Your home will be the primary source of their religious education because it will be your example that they will follow in their early years. As they grow into adulthood they will make their own decision with regard to God and the religion of their choice.

Seeking help from legitimate ministers of religious faiths is a wise thing to do. There are few people who can competently seek religious truth without help from those who have spent their lives in the study of religion.

Statistics on marriage verify that those couples who actively participate in the religious faith of their choice will have a far better chance of succeeding in their marriage relationship.

Many couples want their marriage to be performed in the church of their choice. These couples should remember that if they do this, then they are asking God's blessing on their marriage. God will impart His blessing on them in the house of worship they have chosen. He will expect that they, in return, will keep coming to Him in this house of worship and follow the tenets of faith that they agreed to by coming to Him in this sacred place.

RELIGION QUESTIONS

Will you accept the Ten Commandments as an authority in your life?

The Ten Commandments are universal in their appeal as the spoken laws of nature and God. All religions, no matter what denomination, believe in a form of these commandments.

The first three commandments recognize the existence of God:

> I am the Lord thy God; thou shalt not have strange gods before Me.
> Remember thou keep holy the Sabbath day.
> Thou shalt not take the name of the Lord thy God in vain.

The remaining seven set forth a code of conduct by which men should live their lives:

> Honor thy father and thy mother.
> Thou shalt not kill.
> Thou shalt not commit adultery.
> Thou shalt not steal.
> Thou shalt not bear false witness against thy neighbor.
> Thou shalt not covet thy neighbor's wife.
> Thou shalt not covet thy neighbor's goods.

If you accept these commandments as the code of conduct by which you and your spouse will conduct your married life with one another, it gives you a guide by which you can have assurance of how you will behave toward one another. Your partner can rely on the fact that you believe in God and that you will not lie, steal, or commit adultery. Both of you agree to set aside one day of the week for religious worship. The acceptance of this rule of conduct between you also assumes that if you break any of these rules you will seek forgiveness of God and renew your commitment to keep these commandments.

Those people who value their religious faith are grateful for these commandments for the guidance they give in making decisions affecting their lives. They will recognize that sin and vice are an obstacle to the two of them becoming one. Mortal sin is always a complete barrier to the two ever becoming one in mind, emotion, and spirit.

Do you believe in a Supreme Being who created all things and to whom man refers as God?

The greatest minds from all generations have examined this question. Most of them agree that our world and its order could not have happened by chance. Most people on earth believe that God exists.

Whether or not you accept this belief is extremely important to you and your partner. If you do not accept it, then your lives will be lived by rules you make up for yourselves and the ones that are made for you by society. Neither of these sources of authority in your lives is able to establish a code of conduct on which you can rely for truth. The rules will always be changing and neither of you can ever be sure what to believe or rely on with the other.

Do you believe that Jesus Christ is the Son of God?

This answer to this question separates the religions of the world immediately. Many people believe that Christ was a great teacher, a great man, but not the Son of God. Christ said that He is. Christians believe that He is Christ, the Second Person of the Holy Trinity.

Jews, Moslems and Buddhists do not believe Christ is the Son of God but all believe in some form of the Ten Commandments.

Christ taught his apostles and disciples Divine Truth that has been imparted to us. If you believe in Him as the Son of God then His teachings will have a profound effect on your marriage to one another.

Do you believe in Heaven? Do you believe in Hell?

The answers to these questions will also determine how you live your lives. People who believe that there is a life after death and that heaven, with the presence of God, is the promised reward for a life of faith and obedience to God's laws will want to obey His commandments.

These people also believe that there is a hell where people are punished who refuse to live their lives based on the commandments of God. When you accept these beliefs then a third person enters your marital union, God. Now you are no longer responsible only to each other for the manner in which you handle your relationship. You become responsible for the life of the soul of your partner and your partner for yours. How important is this responsibility? The *Talmud* answered this question more than 1500 years ago.

"Therefore was a single man only first created to teach thee that whosoever destroys a single soul from the children of man, Scripture charges him as though he had destroyed the whole world."

If you answer that you do not believe in heaven and hell then the special qualities attributed to "soul" are removed from your relationship. You do not recognize any authority outside yourself for your personal conduct. Your marriage may be regarded only as a civil contract that you can break whenever you feel like it. It is extremely important to find out these beliefs before you enter into a relationship as intimate and difficult as marriage.

Did your parents teach you a particular religious faith?

If they did, it will probably form the basis from which you shape your adult religious views. You will not ordinarily stray from the religious path on which your parents set you without some great motivation. It is important for your partner to know whether or not you learned the doctrines of your faith and follow their teachings. If you learned these you will probably want your children to learn them too. It is important that you and your partner come to some agreement as to the religious views you will teach your children.

Do you believe marriage vows made before God in church are permanent until death?

Your answer may determine the strength you bring forth in working out the problems that will inevitably result from your marriage. If you believe your vows are permanent, you will try to work out any difficulties in an amicable way.

Even if you cannot you will not seek to make new vows with another person as long as your spouse is living.

If you do not believe they are permanent, the commitment you give to your partner may contain reservations that could annul your marriage. You may also have a lower tolerance for solving any problems between you if they become more than you wish to contend with. Making new vows with another person will be just as hard to keep and you may continue the pattern of walking out rather than solving what is wrong. In any case, your partner has a right to know your views.

Were you married in a church ceremony?

If you were, the commitment you made to each other and the religious community you chose to perform your wedding should become a dominant force in your lives. If your commitment to each other was sincere, you will act in a new way at all times that can be interpreted as acting in unison with each other and the religious community you chose. Just as you join with each other in working for your marriage, you will also join with other members of your religious community in their efforts to practice their faith.

If your commitment was insincere, you will quickly fall away from the religious community and you may develop the habit of seeking your own way with your partner. Your partner will be able to discern your intentions rather quickly and so will your religious community. Both your partner and your religion can help you grow and mature the way an adult should if you let them.

Religion

Do you believe God was actually present at your ceremony?

Marriage vows made before God in His church are sacred. God will always keep His vows to you as a married couple to help you sustain your vows to each other when it becomes hard to do so. God wants you to maintain your spiritual life in good order and will give you the necessary grace to do so if you ask Him.

It is often difficult to tell whether or not a couple making vows in church are sincere in their commitment to God regarding their spiritual life, or, if the church is being used for social and ceremonial purposes. Your actions after the wedding is over will quickly reveal your intentions. Faithfulness to God is equivalent to faithfulness to each other. The opposite may also be true.

Do you attend church regularly?

If your commitment to your faith was sincere, you will want to maintain your spiritual life through weekly renewal with the rest of your community. This is what God commanded when He said, "Remember to keep holy the Sabbath Day."

If your commitment was insincere you will quickly fall away from the habit of church attendance each week because you will not consider your spiritual life important enough to follow through with your presence.

Do you support your religious beliefs with regular contributions?

Churches exist for the purpose of public worship of people who believe in their religious faith. They want a place where they can gather and express their adoration in a public way. Ministers, priests, rabbis and gurus must depend on the willing support of their flock in order to maintain these houses of worship and to support themselves in the work they do for their people. If you partake of the services, then it should be your habit to support your religion.

If your religious views differ, are you willing to accommodate the views of your partner?

In marriages where religious faiths differ, accommodations are always necessary if there is to be peace and harmony in the home. It is also necessary to decide the religious faith in which the children will be reared. This may require patience and tolerance the entire time of the marriage.

If both partners are fervent about their religious faiths, then tense, fragile feelings must be dealt with tenderly if deep hurt is to be avoided. The soul or spirit of each person is that realm over which no one has a right to exercise control. It is the place where you can be hurt deeply. It is the only place where your partner does not have the right to invade without your permission.

If your views differ and one of you is not particularly fervent, he or she may be more easily convinced to let the partner's religious views prevail and thereby avoid many of the conflicts that would otherwise arise. Even so, the quiet ease present when two people are joined in the same faith will not be available to the two of you.

Religion

Are you willing to "give up" your religion for your partner?

If you answer yes to this question you must ask yourself how sincere is your religious belief. Since your religious faith involves God, you should be very careful that you are not also "giving up" God in your life.

Some accommodation may need to be made so that you can maintain your religion and still marry the person you love. No one has the right to ask you to "give up" your religion, even for a marriage commitment. The advent of children, and the choice of the religious faith in which they will be raised, will require a sacrifice on the part of one partner. It is a matter of great importance and should be discussed thoroughly with each other.

If there is a conflict, do you want your children to learn your religion rather than those of your partner?

A choice is inevitable or the children will learn nothing. The moral education you should impart will be missing. It will deeply affect their lives. Children are one of the principal reasons why parents should hold the same religious faith. If you cannot have this in your marriage, then one partner will live with a disturbed conscience at all times. This cannot help but affect your marriage relationship. It is a matter that must be discussed over and over again to avoid the spiritual hurt that will be felt.

9

COMMUNITY

Every couple entering marriage becomes a new family unit that is affected by, and is a part of, a worldwide community that expresses itself in the area and neighborhood of their residence. The community speaks to all its citizens through the laws it makes for providing a standard of conduct for them. Of necessity, everyone will not be pleased with all laws of the community all of the time. But these laws do mean that an authority outside of yourselves will be exercised over you.

Each community makes special laws that give definition to the rights and obligations of being married. Laws relating to children, property, taxes, inheritance of estates, financial obligation and support of spouses and children, are all unique in the married state. All communities look with favor on marriage and will usually bestow special privileges and advantages to married couples.

In a republic like the Unites States of America, elected representatives of the people make the laws of the city, state and nation. These representatives, by their majority vote, make these laws for the orderly living of all citizens. The method of citizen participation in this process is through community politics. Though this subject is utterly essential to your lives, it can generate intense friction through discussion. Political agreement in your marriage may be hard to come by and is not entirely necessary for a successful marriage. Though political disagreement may pose its problems, it is certainly tolerable in the best of marriages.

Politics will exert such an influence in your lives that it will determine many of your expenses with regard to home ownership or rent, educational facilities for your children, and community standards by which you will be expected to live.

The personal character of the people your community elects to set these standards will be reflected in all areas of your daily living. Hardly any aspect of your married lives will go untouched by political influence. Your personal character will, in turn, have an influence on the politics of your community. Each community reflects the personal character of its citizens in the representatives they choose.

You have been, and will be, indelibly marked by the country of your birth and it will have a unique place in your life always. The people and their politics are what gives each country its special flavor.

If you, as a couple, and others in your community, are apathetic and uncaring about your political lives, they will be influenced by those who are not. Your place in your community and its politics are worthy of much attention and discussion between husband and wife.

COMMUNITY QUESTIONS

Have you studied the history of your country?

Schools you attended should have had courses in the history of your country. These courses provide you with just the basic information you need to be able to live in your community. It is amazing to listen to "man-on-the-street" type of interviews and to learn how lacking in knowledge many people are of the history of their country. It may be equally interesting when the two of you discuss this subject.

Do you appreciate the heritage your forefathers handed down to you?

The sacrifice of lives and property through many generations have been made in order for you to live in the freedom afforded to every citizen in the United States of America. Appreciating this heritage is basic to enjoying the privileges you have.

Are you proud of your country?

Pride in your country means that you have learned about it and have feelings of love for it even though you know both the good and bad that exist in it.

Do you like living in this country?

The opportunity to live your lives with as little interference as possible from the government in order to live in peace and harmony with other citizens should be the goal of everyone. If you feel that another country would give you more opportunity to achieve this goal then you may be dissatisfied living here. Surely you must see how important it is for your partner to know your feelings in this regard. How you feel about your country is a matter to be discussed between you so that you will have a harmony of minds about this subject.

Do you believe you have a voice in the government of your country?

If you do, then you will know that you have the power to join with others of your community to make those changes that you believe are necessary for a better life for yourself and your children. If you do not, then you will tend to be apathetic and allow your government to rule you without your voice being heard. You should discuss your feelings on this subject with each other.

Are you interested in politics?

Some people are content to ignore the role politics plays in their lives and let politicians do whatever they want without any influence from them as citizens. Other citizens want to exercise as much control over politicians as they can in order to have a voice in what happens to them and their country. In a marriage these two viewpoints may be held by both of you. Deciding whether you will be able to tolerate this difference cannot happen unless you discuss it.

Do you vote in local, state and national elections?

This is the minimum level of interest that all citizens display in the politics of their government. The lowest level of all is when citizens fail to vote. Many citizens in this country display the lowest level. If you do not vote, you give your political power to others who do vote. Not voting is voting for others to vote for you. Discuss with each other how you feel about this.

Do you know how a political party works?

You will not be able to understand the forces affecting you through politics if you do not gain some knowledge about how a political party functions. Not everyone is inclined or obliged to actively take part in running for elective office or even to actively work for their political party preference. However, all citizens should know how a political party operates and how it chooses a list of candidates. You will be asked to vote for these people to represent you in the legislative and executive branches of your state and federal government. Therefore, it is in your interest to know how they are chosen.

Do you have a preferred political party?

If you do not, and you fail to register with one, you will be unable to exercise a voice in primary elections that may go on within each party for selection of candidates for public office. It is a compelling reason for choosing one rather than being an independent voter. Yet, some citizens feel so strongly that they do not want to align themselves with any political party that they willingly give up this right.

Would you be a candidate for public office?

If you think you would be a candidate, then this subject is of vital importance to your spouse. Newspapers and magazines abound with stories of the difficulties inherent in marriages where either the husband or wife is an elected public official. This decision can bring the light of publicity into the family's life immediately. Marriage partners must discuss this question in detail. It is a time to realize that your married partner comes before a demand to run for public office. Willing consent to this type of life is essential if the marriage is to succeed.

Have you ever petitioned a political representative to change a law?

The political activity of most citizens will be had on the community level. It would be very difficult for one person to petition their representative to change a law. Laws are made for the benefit of many. Therefore if you wish to change one, then it is important to seek the help and influence of others in your community who share your view.

Do you believe a person must be corrupt to be in politics?

Because of the public nature of holding political office, all abuses are subject to publicity in newspapers, radio, television, and the internet. This opens the possibility of notoriety to political corruption that is not present in other careers. It is true that political power tends to corrupt the office holder but all politicians do not succumb to this temptation. There are always good and bad people functioning in every profession and career. The difference between politicians and other professions is that if the candidate for public office is corrupt then the people in his district who knew him well failed to prevent his election. We do not have that choice in other careers.

Do you ever disobey a law simply because you think it is unjust?

For some people disobedience to a law is a way of expressing dissatisfaction with it. When there are a sufficient number of people who disagree with a law and ban together to deliberately disobey it they set a bad

Community

example for all of us. Their proper recourse is to ban together to change the law so that disobedience will not be necessary.

As a rule, are you respectful toward policeman?

Policemen are the visible manifestation of the laws made for our good and protection. Your attitude toward them will reveal your inner feelings about these laws. Policemen are needed because not all citizens will obey the laws of their community. Policemen put their lives on the line for all of us and for this reason deserve our respect.

Do you generally obey traffic laws?

These are the laws made for the safety of all people who travel on the roads and highways of our country. Your respect for these laws will reveal your attitude toward others who use these roads and highways with you. Obeying simple laws, like traffic safety ones, can quickly reveal your level of maturity. If you become impatient and enraged with your fellow travelers, you show that you are immature and not yet ready for a marriage relationship.

Have you ever deliberately neglected to pay a tax bill?

Tax bills are assessed for services made to the community by government. If you deliberately refuse to pay your share of the expense for these services, then you are expecting others to carry your share of the burden. If you are dissatisfied with the government over the amount of money spent for services to the people then join with others to show your discontent and make a change come about with your combined voices.

Are you honest regarding your income tax returns?

Income tax laws became effective in this country in the twentieth century. We did not always have them. Therefore, these particular laws can be the cause of hot dispute. Nevertheless, elected representatives enacted the income tax laws and everyone is obliged to obey them. If you don't like them, and most people don't, then join with other citizens to express your dissatisfaction to your elected representatives who have the power to change these laws. Cheating on your income tax return is a dangerous course to follow and it reveals a flaw in your character that will be evident to the most important person in your life, your married partner.

Have you ever been arrested? Served a jail sentence? Been in court for any reason?

If the answer is "yes" to any of these questions then your marriage partner has a right to know this and you have an obligation to reveal it and discuss it thoroughly. It will affect your marriage relationship.

Have you served in the Armed Forces?

If the answer is "yes" then you need to reveal to your partner in marriage what kind of work you did in the military service and what rank you attained. This should be discussed in detail. It is amazing to learn how many married couples have not discussed this vital information with one another.

The greatest regard one can show for one's country is to serve in the Armed Forces. This is done for the protection of all citizens but it is also a sacrifice of time, effort and youthful years for your fellow man. In the performance of this service in wartime you may have experienced battles that you feel hesitant to discuss with anyone because of the private and painful nature of them. But your married partner is the one person who must have this information in order to "know" the whole person he or she is married to.

Did you finish your enlistment or draft period?

If for some reason you did not, then your spouse must have this information. It may be an indication of the regard you hold for a commitment you have made. If you had a good reason for not finishing your enlistment or draft period then your married partner needs to know why this happened.

What kind of discharge did you receive?

Your marriage partner has a right to know the answer to this question. If it was honorable, you will be happy to reveal it but if it was not, you have an obligation to let your partner know why not.

Would you refuse to serve in the Armed Forces?

There are some pacifists who genuinely feel that the use of force in settling disputes is always wrong. A sincere conviction in this regard will be reflected in other actions as well, e.g., truthful dislike for violence in any form, unwillingness to kill for any reason, conviction that war is unnecessary and unjust, willingness to serve the community in a peaceful way rather than a violent one. Alongside the genuine pacifist, however, are those who do not want to sacrifice the precious youthful years that a draft might require. Looking behind the words for actions will usually distinguish one from the other.

How do you feel about others who refuse to serve?

This will reveal whether or not you are able to tolerate the genuine pacifist and understand his or her feelings.

Do you believe in saluting the flag?

The flag is the outward symbol of inward respect for your country. Saluting it is an outward manifestation of your inward regard. If you refuse to salute the flag then your reason needs to be explained to your partner in marriage. He or she lives in the same country and may share opposite feelings.

Would you use the flag of your country in a way that might be considered disrespectful?

If so, you go a step further than refusing to salute the flag. This shows contempt for your country by using its symbol to express your lack of esteem. It also shows a lack of maturity in knowing how to express your dissatisfaction. Your partner may then wonder if you are mature enough for a marriage relationship.

WORLDWIDE COMMUNITY

The technological advances in the last half of the twentieth century in the field of communications have produced an awareness of the individual's sense of belonging to a worldwide community never before realized. Though a few attempts have been made in the past to cause this awareness to come about, nothing has had the impact that television has produced – not even two world wars involving many countries simultaneously.

Now the citizens of the world watch wars being fought, the degradation of poverty being lived, the slow, painful death hunger produces, and the diseases that could be cured -- on a television screen. It has been said that a picture is worth a thousand words, but it is also more convincing than a war. The conscience of the world is enlightened in an unforgettable way. It is stirred beyond the power of war to produce. It is pricked for action to be taken in order for peace of soul to be restored.

This peace will never come until efforts have been made to love our worldwide neighbors as ourselves. This peace we seek cannot be realized until a worldwide method of non-violent settlement of boundary disputes between nations is agreed upon. As a world community we need to agree to speak a common language. The production and distribution of food needs to be planned on an earth-wide basis. People all over the world need to be able to use the natural resources found in each country. All persons need to have medicines available to them when they are sick.

Man began from a family of one man and one woman. We must return to the idea this entails: being one family of Man. This is the ultimate community.

10

EDUCATION

In the course of growing from one age to another, we are able to learn about ourselves, about the world we live in, and life in general. There is much knowledge that can be acquired simply by being observant to what is going on around us. This requires each of us to be a person who thinks about what is happening around him or her each day. This kind of education takes place in the classroom of our environment. It is not formal education but learning nevertheless.

Many traditions that have endured from one generation to the next have come down to us, not because of some great philosopher or thinker, but rather, from people applying common sense to their lives. Some people seem to be especially blessed with a great deal of this "common sense" while others seem to lack it completely. The lack of it can be disastrous in a marriage relationship.

The opportunity to gain the most knowledge over the shortest period of time is given through formal education in schools of learning. In centuries past, only wealthy persons were afforded this opportunity. When America was founded as a nation, our forefathers believed that in order for the republic to survive, the citizens must be educated. Therefore, schools for children to attend at an early age were established. Now, most countries of the world want to provide education for children from a very early age.

Reaction to formal education is unique to each person. Parents can send the child to school and teachers can impart knowledge, but the child determines how much of this knowledge he or she will absorb in his or her mind. There is a difference between attending school and learning. One is fulfilling the requirement of having your body present in the classroom, and the other is opening the mind to learning the lessons being taught. Obedience determines the ability of the child to open his or her mind to what the teacher is trying to teach.

Without obedience from students, teachers are thwarted and frustrated in their attempts to impart knowledge. When you attended school you were put in an atmosphere whereby you were required to make a commitment that you wanted to grow in maturity and learn how to be a productive adult. The degree of this commitment was the first determination of whether or not you wanted to become a mature person.

Therefore, much can be learned about the adult by looking backward at the response he or she made to educational opportunities presented to him or her. If the commitment was shallow and the student did not learn and progress normally in this educational setting, then the marriage partner should look closely at the commitment this person is claiming to make in a marriage relationship.

To a great extent, your education, and that of your partner, will determine where you live, your standard of living, the manner in which you raise your children, how many children you have, and even the type of friends you will be able to enjoy. Your education forms the basis for your life as an adult person.

Education should not stop at the last graduation from a school or college. It should go on for the rest of your life. The desire "to know" is what life is all about and it is like the desire "to love" – the cup is never full.

EDUCATION QUESTIONS

Do you seem to be able to apply common sense in your life?

If you are blessed with this ability, many decisions will be instinctively made in harmony with the circumstances with which you are presented. No long discussion or considerations about simple things will be necessary for you to make logical decisions. Those without this ability will have difficulty making these. Common sense relieves those blessed with it from asking ""why" to many ordinary facts of life that those without it will be unable to do. Look for this in yourself and your partner

Did you and your partner attend and graduate from elementary school?

Those who successfully complete this milestone in life should have learned how to read, write, add, subtract, multiply and divide rather well. They should also have learned something about the geography and history of the country and the world. It comes as no surprise to teachers in secondary schools that this does not always happen. It sometimes comes as a great surprise to a married partner. The ability to do these things well is of crucial importance to you as a married couple. Do not take the answer for granted – ask it.

Did you and your partner attend and graduate from secondary school?

High school years are spent in preparation for adulthood. They are frequently tumultuous years because the problems of adolescent growth are met at the same time young people are trying to prepare for the manner in which their adult life will be lived. These years present each person with a deep need to make personal decisions apart from their parents and teachers. However, dependence on both parents and teachers make this need a difficult one to balance. How you handled these years is of prime importance to your partner in marriage. Though each of you will mature and grow in your marriage, these years are the first indication of how you handle intimate problems in your life.

Have you discussed your attitudes about school with one another?

Your partner will be deeply interested in learning about a part of your life that he or she does not know if you did not grow up in the same locality. Your partner has a right to know the answers to these questions. Did you enjoy school or did you hate it? Did you do well in your subjects or poorly? Did you ever "stay back" or skip a year? Were you bored with school and your teachers? Did you win any honors or scholarships? Did you deliberately skip classes or cheat on your exams? Did you work after school at a part-time job? Did you play sports? Did you enjoy relationships with other students? The answers to these questions reveal a great deal about your maturity. They also tell much about the person you now are.

Did you attend your graduation ceremony?

Some young people nowadays do not see the benefit in attending their graduation ceremony. They only want the diploma. Yet a graduation ceremony is the expression of tribute paid for work done by you over a long period of time and also to your parents, teachers and the society that provided the education for you. It is part of the reward for labors expended by many people. If you refused to participate in the honor of the ceremony, those persons who helped you achieve this education are prohibited from participating too. In effect you are being inconsiderate by cheating them of a right they have.

There are those who do not enjoy receiving the awards of life and are content with letting others participate in the rituals of tradition while they do not. They feel perfectly justified in doing this because they do not enjoy it. The effect on others involved is of no consequence. A graduation ceremony may be an indication of how other rituals in your life will be celebrated by you and your partner, such as birthdays, anniversaries, weddings and other holidays. Take a look at what your attitude was at the first ceremony over which you had control, your graduation from high school.

Do you make practical use of your educational efforts?

This is the first practical test you face regarding your education. Being cultured and having knowledge are sufficient rewards for the effort education requires. But the practical use of your education depends on what you do with the tools you have gained through education. The practicalities of life usually require that you make some financial gain from the education you received. You are now an adult and, hopefully, a mature one. Mature people must work to support themselves minimally. Husbands and wives usually have children to support as well. The practical use of your education is of prime importance to you and your partner. Usually, one of you will be furthering a career outside the home and the other will be rearing and teaching children in the home. Both of these careers are sacrificial ones that are very demanding.

11

CAREER

In no other aspect of your life will your own uniqueness come to the fore as in the sense of fulfillment you are able to achieve from your career. Most of your youth has been spent in trying to help you discover the qualities that make you an individual person. Your career is the method by which you make these talents known to yourself and others. Your success or failure can be propelled or retarded by the person you marry. Your partner will be your ego builder, or destroyer, in achieving your goals. Choose him or her carefully.

When you marry, two careers are joined and you must make them compatible with your married status. The activity of one must benefit the other and this rhythm should be constantly flowing between the two people who are endeavoring to make these careers succeed. Constant attention must be paid to the effect one career is having on the other.

Both husband and wife must always feel that the other is fulfilling inner drives to succeed in accomplishing goals unique to him or her. When either feels caught in a career that is unfulfilling, dispositions and attitudes will be forthcoming that will prevent the harmony necessary to married life.

The selfishness of one in fulfilling his or her needs at the expense of the other will throw this whole rhythm out of kilter and may injure the marriage irreparably. Each partner in the marriage relationship needs encouragement in order to achieve success in the abilities that each believes he or she has. Both will need this for stamina to keep trying in spite of all obstacles. If this is lacking, success may be achieved in spite of the partner, or will not be achieved at all.

Opportunity abounds in your career choices when you are young and decisions begin to be made while you are still in school. When you reach adulthood the variety of choices you are able to make narrows to a very few. Much will depend on the learning and training that was offered and the talent and interest with which you absorbed it.

Obviously your career choice should be attained before the advent of marriage. Trying to combine educational opportunities within the marriage relationship puts strains on the relationship that really do not belong there. Marriage has its own demands as a career and is time and energy consuming. Choosing the right career for you and preparing yourself to do it is almost a "must" before marriage.

Too few people are fortunate enough to be paid for that which they enjoy doing most. This should be the goal of every career choice. Those who are so lucky to have this are fortunate indeed. If it is possible to share this with your marriage partner, you are twice blessed.

Many people are forced to work at boring, unwanted jobs simply for a paycheck. In adulthood, a paycheck often becomes that important. Spending forty hours (or more) every week of your life in this type of endeavor does not always create the kind of disposition and attitude needed for happiness and contentment in marriage. If you are caught in this trap, some plan and much strength will be needed to break the chains of boredom that bind you. It is not easy but it can be done.

If you are trying to do this while you are married, your partner will have to help you with as intense a desire as your own. Both of you need to realize that the thrust with which other marriages are able to move forward will have to be slowed down in yours. You will have to accept this aspect of your married life and work with it and not against it. The striving you do together can bring the two of you to a closeness that other marriages may lack. This can be a most satisfying alternative.

CAREER QUESTIONS

What is your attitude toward work?

This may seem a ridiculous question to ask, yet a prevalent attitude exists whereby some feel that avoidance of work is a career in itself. Nevertheless, those who find contentment and satisfaction for a sense of accomplishment for the work they do are among the happiest people. On the other hand, "clock watchers" or "paper shufflers" are among the most pitiful and boring.

Your attitude toward work determines whether or not you will be a success in your career and your marriage. Both require you to put forth much effort for success to be achieved. Your attitude toward work will be revealed in the daily rituals of your life. If you have to be prodded to get out of bed and arrive for work on time, this may reveal an immature part of your life you should correct. You need to be dependable both on the job and in your marriage. No one should have to prod you to accept responsibility for doing your job.

Do you work in the field in which you want to work?

Your career will affect your life for the longest period of time of any decision you make outside of marriage. You should have already asked yourself what you hope to achieve in performing your life's work.

Some people seek fame and fortune. Others want to work in service to their fellow man. Many people are more talented in working with their "hands" while others prefer "mental" jobs. An artistic nature drives others to seek expression in one of the arts. Whatever your choice of career, if you decide to marry, it must be blended with the needs of the marriage and your marriage partner.

Some determination needs to be made as to whether or not you have the ability to succeed in the career you have chosen. You need to pay attention to your motivation for choosing this field and whether it is a realistic one for you. Sharing dreams and ambitions with the one you love in marriage is very fulfilling and should supply the encouragement you need to go forward in your career. This is a special blessing that married couples have that others do not in being able to share these goals with one another.

Do you want to be an employee or self-employed?

People have distinct desires in this regard. Those who want self-employment usually are never satisfied until they try it. Those who do not want the responsibilities that self-employment entails will seek the security of employment by others. Neither status is ever fully secure. You need to discuss this matter with your partner in marriage because it will be of great consequence to you in your relationship with one another. A person who chooses self-employment will need the understanding and help of the partner more than one who works for an employer.

Are there career choices that either of you have strong objections to the other doing?

The basis for such objections will determine whether they are valid ones or not. Emotions regarding this subject may be so strong that objectivity may be hard to come by. If it is a problem, or becomes one in your marriage, the feelings of one partner are going to be squashed by the other even if agreement is reached. The choice of a career to which your partner has strong objections will produce daily anxiety that is difficult to endure for a lifetime. Your commitment to love each other through every problem you face may be tested but it can also be the biggest asset you have in solving the problem.

Are you willing to go anywhere in the country or world for your career fulfillment?

The uprooting of family ties that this may entail demands agreement by both partners. Losses and gains must be carefully weighed. Emotions that cannot be helped must be dealt with. One cannot go alone and have a meaningful marriage relationship maintained.

Are you willing to "climb the ladder of success" whether your partner approves or not?

Few marriages begin on the premise that this would or could happen. The intense desire to succeed in career goals and the outside pressures that may be applied by career associates and bosses often create a situation where this becomes a problem. The company man or woman who always says "yes" to the boss regardless of consideration to the married partner can easily fall into this pit. A successful marriage depends on your ability to give a proper balance to both career and you marriage partner.

Will you be able to grow with each other in your careers rather than apart?

One of the greatest dangers to marital happiness comes when one partner grows and the other does not keep pace. It often becomes necessary for the growing partner to exercise patience and to give help to the non-growing one in order not to lose sight of each other. Yet growth patterns change from one partner to the other rapidly and you never know when you will be the one who needs this patience and this help exercised on your behalf.

Do both of you believe the husband should be the head of the house and principal provider for the family?

The masculine nature of the husband is such that he is ideally suited to perform this function. His masculinity gives him the right to assume this role. He will be unable to competently fulfill it without the willing consent of his feminine partner. She has the maternal instinct in her nature while the paternal instinct of protector is in his. This is the natural and perfect way that married couples complement each other.

The family will need the father to perform this role for its nourishment and growth. If the father fails to do this, the family will be fragmented and confused because it needs the structure he provides. It needs this for its survival and for the teaching the children need regarding how family life should be lived.

Though the husband has this important role as head of the house, he has an obligation to the family to be sure that he does not act arbitrarily and that all of his decisions affecting them will be made with a loving commitment to them. He must exercise his role as head of the home by seeing to it that all of his decisions are moral, legal, ethical and practical. When the family knows he will use this objective standard they need never fear that he will act in a tyrannical way toward any of them in any situation.

Do you both believe a wife in the home has a career there that is definite and distinctive?

The commitment a woman makes in marriage is like no other on earth. She gives herself to her husband in loving abandon and usually gives up the opportunity for a career outside the home until after the children are raised. She shares his life, complements his nature, and manages the care for their home and children. It is the most difficult, and rewarding, vocation in life. Her feminine nature makes it possible for her to do this. Her maternal instinct is fulfilled in doing it.

In taking on this role, it does not mean that she gives up any of her rights as a person, a free and independent one. But it does mean that she recognizes a need to depend on her husband during the years the children are being raised. If she cannot depend on her husband during these years, then she will be torn in several directions because of the needs of children for a mother in the home. It is the dilemma every single mother knows well.

Are you both willing for the wife to work outside the home during child-rearing years?

In most cases mothers work because the financial rewards are necessary for the standard of living the family needs or desires. Sometimes mothers begin to work for a sense of fulfillment that is lacking in their lives staying home and caring for children. The boredom of housework, or the need to be with other people, may have motivated them in the beginning, but few mothers find life in the world of business so fascinating that they willingly leave the home where young children need to be cared for every day.

12

HEALTH

In matrimony, one of the solemn vows is to love and cherish each other in sickness and in health. Only by taking a few minutes to reflect on this vow can you come to a true realization of the implications in it. To love and cherish – in sickness and in health – can be quite a trial. Sickness can have the effect of drawing two people closer together, but ill health is also a great burden. Not everyone can carry it, but marriage may demand that you try.

Health affects every other aspect of your married life. If you are fortunate enough to have good health, life's pleasures can be enjoyed to the fullest. If you are unfortunate enough to have ill health, life must be coped with on a different basis on all levels of living.

To some extent you are able to predict your own good, or bad, health by knowing the many factors that control your body. Proper diet and exercise are the most important factors in all of your attempts to maintain health of body. Many diseases that could cripple your health can be prevented through inoculation. Illnesses treated in their early stages can result in the restoration of you health and medicines may be able to control illnesses that cannot be cured. All of these health factors are within your control.

If your health becomes poor this can result in argument, strife and tension between you as a married couple. This can happen when the person with poor health adopts an attitude of whimpering, griping and being difficult to live with. Most people want to help someone who is suffering who maintains a good attitude. Strife and tension may also result if the healthy partner does not want to make the sacrifice of his or her life in order to care for their partner. As sad as this situation is, it does happen. Illness can alter the personality of the unhealthy partner as well as the healthy one. The well partner suffers the agony of watching someone they love in pain and suffering. This is a hard thing to do. Both need comfort and inspiration to get through this kind of life.

If illness occurs, both of you need to talk about it in a very open way. This will give each of you the opportunity to help the other with kindness and consideration.

When your marriage lasts many years and you both grow old together, your bodies will begin to deteriorate and illnesses will most likely happen. By this time the bond of love between you will overcome any obstacle that illness will place in your way.

Good health is one of the most precious gifts of life. Treasure it, protect it, and preserve it.

HEALTH QUESTIONS

Does your partner know your true age?

Some people are very sensitive about their age and do not wish to reveal it to everyone who asks. Politeness requires that they be allowed this privilege. However, between married partners it is important that the truth be told. In most marriages this may seem a ridiculous question to ask but in a few it can be a source of deception on the part of one partner for very personal reasons.

Medical forms always ask the date of birth because it is important to know this factor in treating one's health. As we grow older physical changes occur in our bodies. Habits need to be altered to reflect these changes. Women will go through hormonal changes in the body to accommodate her role in conceiving children. These may seriously affect her moods and personality on a temporary basis. Men may have to change their habits with regard to sports and give up some that are too strenuous for their age.

Are you overweight or underweight?

Most couples look at their wedding pictures and smile at the young bride and groom who are slim and trim. But as the years go by weight is added and the body reflects our age and the different life style we now have. It is expected that some weight will be gained as the years go by. How much weight we gain can be a health concern. Obesity is a serious problem in our country. More sedentary life styles, the availability of fast foods, eating out more often, lack of exercise, are all factors that may contribute to this condition. But caring for our health means that we must try to control weight as it can cause so many other health problems, e.g., heart and diabetes.

Volumes of books have been written with regard to weight and weight loss programs abound. But your family doctor is the most valuable source of help if you are overweight.

Underweight can also be a serious problem to one's health. Because the media attempts to brainwash us to believe that our bodies should be "model" slim, women may tend to take this message too far and starve their bodies of the nourishment needed for good health. Serious diseases can result and psychological problems may become a factor. These can be difficult for a marriage partner to contend with.

Overweight, or underweight, needs to be discussed compassionately between a married couple. If your partner is not happy with your weight because of health concerns, or even appearance, it can be affecting your marriage relationship. If it is, you should try to go on the hard road to doing something about it.

Have you had the usual childhood diseases and inoculations?

Mumps, chickenpox, measles and German measles, usually referred to as childhood diseases, can be very serious when contracted as an adult. All are highly contagious. Mumps can cause sterility in a male, chickenpox can leave scars on the skin, measles can cause a rheumatic heart disease, or German measles can cause retardation to an unborn child when the mother contracts the disease while carrying a baby.

Because these diseases are so contagious, most children get them and suffer no severe consequences. However, now there are inoculations that are available to prevent most of these diseases and it is important for parents to consult their doctor about giving these inoculations to their children. Almost all parents have their children inoculated against the most serious diseases such as diphtheria, typhoid, whooping cough, smallpox and polio. All of these can be serious and may cause death. They caused plagues for centuries until inoculations were discovered that have, for the most part, wiped these diseases from the face of the earth.

It is amazing that any parent would fail to have their child inoculated against these diseases but it happens in more alarming numbers each year. Because these diseases have not been a serious health threat for so many years, some parents do not consciously think it is important any longer. Ask your partner if he or she has had these inoculations as a child.

Has either of you ever been hospitalized? Had a permanent injury? Had a disease that left you with limitations to your health?

In the course of growing up, children often sustain injuries that quickly heal. However, some may result in a permanent injury and not be visibly noticeable. A disease may cause a lasting limitation on the activities one is able to do and enjoy. While this information may not need to be revealed to everyone, it is vitally important to your marriage partner. If you do not reveal this information then your partner is unable to understand a part of your life that is important to you. Ask these questions and be open and honest in revealing the answers.

Will each of you take care of your health without being nagged by the other?

One of the most tedious tasks a married partner can encounter is taking care of a husband or wife who will not seek medical help. This type of person will then be a constant complainer about not feeling well. One of the saddest sights in the world is to see a widow or widower wandering through the rewarding years of life without the companionship of a partner who died through neglect of taking care of his or her health.

Regular physical examinations can lengthen your life span because many conditions and diseases can be cured. Your doctor will be able to recommend changes in your lifestyle that will help you to not only live longer but to enjoy the benefits of good health. One of the greatest benefits to be gained by regular physical check-ups is the serenity that comes in knowing you do not have health problems that need attention.

If sterility is a problem, will each of you seek medical help?

Most couples will want children as a result of their loving marriage relationship. This is natural and instinctive. But there are couples who are unable to conceive a child and this can be a serious problem for one or both.

Most people marry without the knowledge of whether they can conceive a child or not. If this knowledge is known before the advent of marriage, this information is vitally important to your intended partner. It is a serious obligation to reveal this.

Medical advances have made it possible for doctors to be able to help couples who believe they are unable to conceive a child. If this is a problem in your marriage, you should discuss this subject openly and honestly with each other in a compassionate way and determine whether or not medical treatment is an option for you to try to investigate.

Is either of you inclined to be homosexual?

It is extremely unfair to a marriage partner to enter into a marriage relationship when one partner has tendencies to homosexuality. By the time most couples reach an age to marry, any person who has a tendency toward homosexuality will know it. To enter a marriage relationship without revealing this fact to your intended partner is very unfair. It will cause great emotional strain in the marriage relationship. It is not uncommon for the homosexual person to have a love affair with another person of the same sex. This obviously will cause great frustration to the married partner. It can cause his or her health, both physically and emotionally, to be at stake. It will usually result in the breakdown of the marriage completely.

Has either of you ever been treated by a psychiatrist or a child psychologist? Confined to a mental hospital? Had a nervous breakdown or attempted suicide?

Outside of the spirit, the mind (or brain) is the most fragile part of the human being. It controls all activity every moment of every day. If mental health is impaired all of the person suffers seriously. Your marriage partner needs to know of any limitations that may cause injury to your mental health. If you have ever had a nervous breakdown or attempted suicide, then your partner should know this in order to understand your fragile nature in this regard. If a psychiatrist has ever treated you for a mental problem, or you have been confined to a mental hospital for any reason, you have an obligation to reveal this to the person you hope to live with in a marriage relationship for the rest of your life.

Does either of you have religious convictions that influence health decisions?

If you have beliefs that would require you to refuse a blood transfusion for yourself, or your child, or to refuse to have children inoculated against childhood diseases, then you owe it to your partner to reveal this belief before marriage. If you would refuse a needed operation for yourself, or your child, this could cause serious strain on the marriage relationship. If you would abort a child that has already been conceived, your partner in marriage needs to know this fact too. These beliefs can result in very serious consequences, not only to the life of your marriage, but to the lives of yourself and your children.

SELF-INDUCED DISEASES

There are certain diseases that require an act of your will to contract. This means that they are avoidable. But, if they are contracted, each is either curable or can be arrested. In each instance the disease cannot be cured without a further act of your will. Each is damaging to your marriage relationship and if no act of the will is forthcoming to cure or arrest the disease then the consequences will probably destroy your marriage.

Has either of you ever had a venereal disease?

Blood tests are required of citizens in the United States seeking marriage licenses. The purpose of this test is to determine whether or not either partner has a venereal disease. If the disease is found, the person must be cured before a license will be issued.

Those who do not engage in premarital sexual relations will not have a venereal disease. Those who have had premarital sexual relations run the risk of contracting one of the many strains of this virus. After marriage, if the married partners have sexual relations only with each other, they need never fear contracting a venereal disease. If, at any time, either partner should abandon their marital vow and have sex with another person they, too, run the risk of contracting a venereal disease. If this happens and the married couple continue to live together, then a new blood test should be sought by both partners to determine whether either one has a disease.

Nature protects the right of married couples to live free of guilt and disease in having sexual intercourse with each other. Nature may punish those who live their lives with sexual promiscuity as a code of their moral conduct. Venereal diseases should be considered serious health hazards as they can cripple your good health and sometimes cause your death.

Is either of you an alcoholic? Is there a history of alcoholism in your family?

Alcoholism is one of the most serious medical problems the world over. Being married to an alcoholic tremendously interferes with the serenity that should be available in your marriage. It destroys family unity and happiness. If it becomes an acute problem, married life becomes so intolerable that the marriage will eventually die because of the alcoholic who will not admit to being one and get help. This disease absolutely requires such an admission before an arrest of the disease is possible. Your partner in marriage cannot do this for you but he or she can be of great assistance in helping you overcome this addiction.

Has either of you ever taken addictive drugs, other than by prescription from a doctor? Have you become addicted to such drugs?

Taking any kind of drug, other than one prescribed by a physician for a disease or injury, is foolish and unwise. It tempts injury to the mind, body, emotions and spirit – the whole person. It will inevitably do harm to others and most especially to your marriage partner. Even prescribed drugs can be a danger because some people may become addicted to them.

Doctors spend many years of study learning about the causes of illness and the manner in which one drug or another may have a beneficial effect on an illness or injury. Yet people, the world over, have decided in alarming numbers that they can safely take drugs without even being sick. This has led to an epidemic of drug addiction. These illegal drugs are being tested on those who are gullible enough to seek them out on the criminal market throughout the world. The results of these tests are found in the emergency rooms of hospitals and in the streets of every city. It is not a pretty picture.

No one should be a human guinea pig in this most grotesque of medical experiments being conducted by drug purveyors. You must commit a criminal act in order to volunteer. Drug addiction is disastrous in a marriage relationship. It will affect the way the whole family is forced to live. Help for this disease is available but the addicted person must be willing to seek treatment in order to overcome the addiction. If the addicted person does not seek this help, the marriage relationship will probably die.

Does either of you smoke cigarettes?

Medical evidence exists in abundance about the serious health problems brought on by people who smoke cigarettes over a long period of time. Though smoking is not considered a disease it can be the cause of many diseases that seriously affect your health.

Smoking is the one addiction that can lead to health problems and have no beneficial effect in its use. Sexual relations between a husband and wife are a proper use of sex. Alcohol used in moderation by those who are able to control the use of it is enjoyable and even good for your health. Drugs used by a doctor for the treatment of disease is beneficial. Tobacco alone is an addiction that has no value in its use.

Addiction to tobacco is usually acquired in youth. Adults will not usually become addicted to tobacco after they have reached an age of sufficient maturity to know its deleterious effects. Cigarette companies advertise extravagantly hoping to entice the young people into this addictive habit for the sake of future profits. Smoking tobacco has become a puberty right in our culture that is supposed to make the youth feel that he or she has reached a point in their growing up process that entitles them to make this decision for themselves. Cigarette companies know the addictive quality of their product and believe that if they can get the youth addicted he or she will carry it on into adulthood, sometimes for the rest of their lives. The use of tobacco can cause serious health problems and is not worth the risk taken.

In addition to the health problems, the expense of the cigarettes, the personal cleanliness of mouth and breath, the air in rooms filled with smoke, and burns in furniture and clothing, combine to make smoking an undesirable habit and one to try to break.

Marriage partners can be of invaluable aid in helping one another to break this bad habit. They can also be a stumbling block if they insist on smoking when one partner is trying to quit. Talk about your attitudes toward smoking tobacco and try to give each other the necessary help to stop if it is a problem in your marriage relationship.

13

FINANCES

Almost every married couple would place finances at, or near, the top of any list of marital problems. Yet, all too humanly, couples contemplating marriage are convinced that their "love" will carry them through all their troubles, including any financial ones. Both attitudes have a certain ring of truth to them. However, facing the true financial facts of life can actually mean success or failure in marriage.

But finances do not depend solely on the amount of money you have, or are making. The decisions you have made regarding the opportunities that presented themselves in your lives determine your ability to earn a livelihood. The answers you have arrived at as a result of analysis of other aspects of your life give a definite answer to where your real financial strength lies.

Your attitude, good and bad, toward yourself and others, has determined your PERSONAL CHARACTER. The generations of cooperation among members of your family, or lack of it, have determined your FAMILY AND HERITAGE background. The moral standards you have decided to live by have culminated in the RELIGION you intend to practice. The strengths and weaknesses of the condition of the world you are inheriting, COMMUNITY, have had a real impact on the way you are able to live. The real knowledge you have acquired and your ability to use it comes from the EDUCATION you received and your use of it. The field in which you work and your ability to gain financial satisfaction and personal fulfillment from it is your CAREER. Your ability to soar freely with a healthy body, or to be limited by one affected by disease or injury, is a factor in your life that determines the status of HEALTH.

Your response to all of the aspects of your life revealed by the answers to these topics, show the level of your maturity and your morality. Your financial opportunities will be determined by many of the decisions you have made in regard to all of these subjects. You have already received the greatest inheritance you will ever be endowed with and you have determined, in great measure, the wealth of this inheritance by the decisions you have made regarding your life. You have chosen whether or not you wanted an education; whether or not you want to work; whether or not you will live peacefully with other people in your community; and whether or not you will accept a moral code of conduct outside yourself to guide you through life. And now you have brought this inheritance into your marriage.

Each of you has brought distinct characteristics into your marriage that will determine the level of maturity and morality with which your marriage relationship will be lived. All of these characteristics determine your ability to gain the financial resources to get the things necessary for your well being, and some of your desires that require money to obtain. Realistic thinking about finances deeply concern both partners in a marriage and a mature attitude about what you can afford, or not, will bring lasting happiness to you as a couple.

If you concentrate too heavily on the things money can buy in the early years of marriage, you may stifle growth in the direction of those virtues money cannot buy. The love shared by you as a couple can make the growth of virtue a rewarding experience. Never forget that moral virtue is more important than financial gain.

Though finances will determine the brilliance with which the many facets of your life will sparkle, you should never forget that such rare and beautiful gifts as love, honor and trustworthiness cannot be bought at any price and are the precious ingredients in any worthwhile marriage. Once you have these, financial success, or lack of it, will not spoil the goodness of your marriage relationship.

All during your marriage both of you will be able to advance the level of your maturity and improve your moral virtues because you should be constantly helping one another grow in both of these directions.

FINANCE QUESTIONS

If both husband and wife work, are you willing to save an amount equal to the wife's income?

If both husband and wife work for monetary compensation, financial success is almost assured. The advent of a child will change this pattern drastically. If you are not willing to save an amount equal to the wife's income, then you may be setting up a standard of living that a child would seriously disrupt. You need to discuss your attitude should this occur. A child cannot be weighed on a financial scale, yet this may happen if you do not plan for the advent of one.

Is the husband earning sufficient income to take care of the financial needs of the marriage?

The key word here is "needs" of your marriage, not desires or wants. It is important to the husband's sense of self-esteem that he be able to do this. When he cannot, or does not, it affects the wife's ability to function in her role. Setting up a standard of living that is realistic to your ability to live on the husband's income is very necessary. This does not preclude the wife working outside the home for monetary gain, but this should never supersede the husband's sense of providing for his wife and family.

Are you willing to live with a budget?

A budget is a very revealing diary about the way you handle your money. All newly married couples need to start out married life by setting up a budget for the manner in which they intend to spend their money. This brings great benefits to their marriage relationship. If you refuse to budget, it may mean that you do not wish to come to grips with the answers a budget would reveal. Budgeting may sound simple and be quickly agreed to, but it requires great strength of will to adhere to one. Sufficient amounts must be set aside for such necessary items as providing shelter, food, utilities and clothing for each other. Transportation, entertainment, cosmetics, medical, dental, charities and insurance may come as shocks and difficult problems to those who did not consciously think about and plan for them. Only after paying for these necessary items of life can you hope to be able to save or purchase extras that you would like to enjoy. The knowledge gained from budgeting can be surprising and helpful to you in getting these.

Even after many years of marriage a budget can help a married couple exercise self-control over spending. It will reveal impulsive and compulsive buying habits quickly. Extravagant tastes will be scrutinized and wasteful buying will hurt when the item is not used or thrown out. The reward of self-control is worth the sacrifices and endeavors it takes to keep a budget. On the other hand, budgeting should not take the joy out of life.

Are you willing to be completely open with one another about your income and expenditures?

Money earned when you are married is a combined effort at all times, regardless to which partner the check is made payable. Neither partner could reasonably give the necessary time to a career without the help of the other and still enjoy the benefits of marriage. If you have ever made an application for a loan you will realize the extent of revelation of your personal financial life that goes into such a form. It is surprising how many husbands and wives will not be as open with one another about finances as they are on an application for a bank loan.

If you argue a lot about money, if you keep separate bank accounts and fail to reveal the amount of money you make, then, for some reason, you do not trust your partner with this information. It may be that you are doing something you do not wish your partner to know or that your partner will not be trustworthy with the information if given. Continuing your marriage relationship, year after year, in this manner, may result in great strain on the marriage. In order to grow close with one another, talking about this most important aspect of marriage is essential.

Are you agreeable about which one of you will handle the money for the family?

You should both agree on which one of you will perform this task. It can be an irksome chore in the attention to detail that it requires. Whether the husband or wife does it, the other partner must be made to feel a part of the business of handling family finances. Unexpected or unplanned expenses can have a whiplash effect on both partners if mature discussion does not take place all of the time. A husband may be made to feel he is an inadequate provider for his family. A wife may begin to feel she is a poor manger of the home. Mature discussion will dispel these emotional fears if they are unfounded – or bring the truth to light if they are valid. Both must manage the money in the marriage relationship but delegation of the details of handling the money should be mutually agreed upon for one to do. Sympathetic understanding should be forthcoming for the delicate effect on the marriage that comes with this task.

Are you willing to consult each other before spending any substantial sum of money?

It should become a habit in your relationship with one another that you always agree to do this. It seems easy to agree to when your emotions are not involved in something you want and you are not under the influence of high-pressure salesmanship. Many couples have learned to their regret that one partner can commit thousands of dollars of the family money by the signature of one partner only. The problem is so prevalent that consumer protection laws have been made to assist those peculiarly subject to salesmanship of this type. If you form a habit of always talking over any unusual expenditure with each other before agreeing to commit yourselves to it, you bring a sense of ease and trustworthiness to your relationship that will benefit it greatly. It can be a good defense against super salesmanship.

Are you satisfied with the manner in which you pay your bills?

Some families do not buy anything unless cash can be paid for it. Others buy many items and pay them out in time payments. You must decide which is the most satisfying way for you to handle the payment of your bills.

If items are bought on time, interest will be a factor to consider in the purchase price. You will pay more but you get the use sooner. You have to decide if this method is worth it. If you choose to pay cash for everything you purchase you may have to wait a very long time for some items to be bought but you will always be in a solvent financial condition.

The manner in which you treat your creditors in the payment of your bills is very telling of your character and maturity. If you are considerate and pay your bills on time, you have learned to exercise control when necessary and not to indulge in new wants until the old ones have been paid for. Merchants who wait for the cash customer will always be solvent but may not sell much. Those who sell to the credit customer may sell more but will have to depend on the good will and consideration of the customer for the payment of the bill. If the merchant receives this, he can be a good friend indeed. Your credit rating will be affected by his report of your conduct.

Couples who do not habitually pay their bills, for whatever reason, learn all kinds of charades in order to avoid talking with their creditors. Wives won't answer the doorbell, telephone numbers are unlisted, and couples move frequently. In general, a calloused attitude is adopted about finances and other aspects of life as well. Not paying bills takes much of the joy out of ordinary living.

Do you habitually spend more money than you have?

The self-control of two people moving in unison is at stake if you habitually spend more money than you make. An agreed upon budget is a must if you are to begin to cope with the problem as a couple. You cannot continue this pattern without serious consequences resulting. Unless you agree to work together to solve the problem, your marriage relationship will be seriously affected.

Do you ever lie to your partner about how much you paid for an item?

If you do, it is yourself you do not trust. There is no need to lie to your partner about this unless you expect disapproval. You do not trust yourself to be able to handle this disapproval. Further, you anticipate it without giving your partner a chance to show whether it would be forthcoming or not. If disapproval is voiced, you must be able to defend your actions if they were valid or change them if they were not.

Do you ever spend money gambling at a casino without your partner's willing consent?

This can be a devastating hurt to the marriage relationship because your partner may feel that you are throwing away the family income if you do. If you are insistent that you be allowed to do this for recreational purposes, then your spouse should agree. If he or she does not agree, then you are putting gambling ahead of your relationship with your partner.

14

RECREATION

Recreation is that time of our lives spent renewing and refreshing our minds, bodies, spirits and emotions. It is the time of fun and games that are the reward for labor. Recreation keeps us from being dull and uninteresting people. Everyone needs recreation time in his or her life and it should happen regularly, frequently and joyously. When you are married it should be wonderfully shared with someone you love. It is hoped that both of you will be able to share these hours together.

The precious hours spent in recreation demands they be spent in as pleasurable a pursuit as possible. Each day should have some recreation time in it. It need not be elaborate in design. Pleasant conversation, in which controversy is avoided, is always enjoyable. Watching a satisfying television show when daily chores are finished is most relaxing. Playing music or reading a good book may be a most satisfying way to spend an evening. Joining with others to play cards or games you enjoy will take your mind away from daily routines. Some sort of recreation time should be consciously planned each and every day. Guard these times from tension and pressure so that it will be true recreation. Otherwise you many not feel the relief that recreation is supposed to bring to your whole body.

The manner of recreation is endless in variety and unique to the talents of each person. It should bring happiness in its pursuit and relaxation in its enjoyment. It is during recreation time that most people meet. Friends are entertained and enjoyed. These are the times when parents spend their happiest moments with their children. Families get together for reunions with one another and joyful conversation and food. Holidays are set aside worldwide for the enjoyment of recreation hours on special days and events.

Just because recreation should be fun it may not always be so. Conflicts of interest may arise and cause arguments to ensue. Vacation time can be especially susceptible to frustration and aggravation if it was not well planned and agreed to beforehand. It would be easy to plan a vacation if you were the only person involved in the endeavor. When a married couple try to do this two different personalities become involved and each one may have likes and dislikes that the other does not share. It sometimes takes a great deal of accommodation just to have a good time. Love and good will toward your partner is the only answer to this dilemma.

RECREATION QUESTIONS

Do you enjoy participating in sports?

The enjoyment of sports is the most common form of recreation and renews all aspects of the total person in their participation. Sports activities shared with your married partner can be particularly pleasing and refreshing. However, it is by no means essential that you enjoy the same sports activities.

Do you spend a lot of time playing sports?

Recreation

Sports activities can consume all of the recreational time of those who enjoy them. If the interest is shared with the married partner, this type of activity can draw two very close. If interest is not shared, some care should be taken lest the two of you grow apart because of the consuming nature sports may engender. The sports enthusiast may not realize the sense of loss this inflicts on the partner who is not so enthusiastic. Asking some basic questions of yourself, and answering them truthfully, should tell you whether or not your sports interests are damaging to your marriage relationship.

Do you spend all of your recreational hours with sports interests?

If this is satisfying to both of you then you will not have a problem with it in your marriage. If it is not pleasing to one of you then you had better talk about it and see if some accommodation can be made to make your marriage first in your lives.

Would you sacrifice a sporting activity to please your partner?

Your partner should always come first. Sports are an extracurricular activity. Your marriage is your life together.

Do you expect your partner to care for children at home alone while you enjoy your sporting activity?

If one partner has this attitude then that person may be seriously damaging the morale of the marriage relationship. If this attitude goes on for a long time, the partner left at home, with the responsibilities that should be shared by two, then that partner cannot help but feel hurt and abandoned.

In order to know the depth of this feeling, the partner who indulges in sporting activities alone week after week, should spend time alone at home with children and household chores. The other partner must then leave and enjoy some activity he or she enjoys alone. Then and only then will you understand the loneliness felt by your partner.

Do you spend a lot of time watching sports events on television?

The interest with which some husbands are able to view sports activities on television is a source of irritation to many wives because of the number of hours this consumes. Further, such events may be scheduled on holidays that create conflicts with traditions that wives may wish for their husbands to participate in as head of the home. Talking about this openly and frankly should bring forth the kind of solution you can both enjoy.

Do you ever gamble on sports? Have you ever won or lost a lot of money gambling? Would you not gamble if your partner did not want you to?

The right of husbands and wives to make reasonable demands on one another would certainly include refraining from spending the family income gambling. Small bets on sporting activities is not usually a problem but if any issue, such as gambling, becomes more important to a partner than the love and consideration due the husband or wife, then the marriage is in serious trouble.

Do you have a hobby?

Hobbies can enhance your interest in the talents you posses and be very fulfilling to your spirit. They are usually

Recreation

creative and make one a more interesting person. A hobby is more of an urge than a necessity. Some people enjoy them and others do not care to have one. Few husbands and wives object to hobbies if reasonable hours are spent on them and the amounts of money they require are within reason.

If you like to create things and enjoy being alone, then find a hobby that will satisfy this desire. Most hobbies involve working with one's hands and doing intricate work. This can be a very fulfilling method of relaxation, especially for people who work with their minds. But a hobby will often involve the investment of time and money, both of which may be unprofitable except in the relaxation and joy you get from indulging yourself by doing something you like.

Do you enjoy dancing? Would you take lessons to learn basic dance steps?

One of the most delightful forms of recreation for some couples is that of going out to dinner, either as a couple or with a group, and dancing afterward. Yet so few husbands and wives will take the trouble to learn basic dance steps in order to share this common form of recreation. The fun, exercise and relaxation that dancing provides can be enjoyed frequently. Further, many activities by groups or clubs are planned around the dinner-dance format. Being able to relax and enjoy dancing during the evening makes you a more pleasing person.

Do you like to attend movies, plays or concerts? Will you accommodate differences of opinion on what to attend?

Attending movies, concerts, or plays, is a pleasurable way to spend recreational hours and these should lift your spirits from the everyday world and bring a sense of relief from daily pressures. They should provide you with an opportunity to get out of the routine of the home without the inconveniences of overnight jaunts. Many movies, plays and concerts are serious "message" shows, though, and if either partner is not in the mood for problem-solving entertainment, care should be taken in the selection of what will be attended.

Do you believe vacations from work are really essential?

Vacations provide families with opportunities to spend time with each other that daily life cannot make possible. The joy of a vacation can be spoiled completely if there is a lack of consideration on the part of married partners. Further, if it becomes necessary to spend vacation time in work activity instead of play, needed relaxation may be put off. Vacations spent this way, year after year, will deprive a couple of needed light-heartedness in their lives.

Are you willing to sacrifice money spent on "things" in order to have a vacation?

The money spent on vacations for a family can be considerable. The temptation to spend this same money on some "thing" that the family needs or would enjoy becomes very great. The release of tension and the relaxation that a vacation should bring is an invisible asset and should not be put off. Lack of getting this release may not show on the individual couple for many years, but it does have an effect that finally becomes visible. The assets to be gained from a vacation are greater than "things" that may be sacrificed for it. This means that you must be willing to save money to be spent this way. Are you?

Do you know the types of vacations you and your partner want to take?

The selection of a place for a married couple to spend vacation time requires thought and cooperation. If children are to be included the place must be carefully chosen to include activities for them. Having fun together can require real work but the work should be in the planning, not in the enjoying. Vacation time can be a sensitive point in determining your ability to accommodate the likes and dislikes of each other.

If a husband and wife share similar interests in their daily life, then planning an enjoyable week or two together without the interference of work can be easily accommodated. But, if husband and wife are in the habit of going separate ways in their activities, it may be difficult to find common ground for planning to spend time together, enjoyably, on a vacation in which mutual interests must be shared.

A family vacation that includes the children requires the ability to set limits on the type of vacation you can have. If the vacation time is to include mutual friends as well, then their personalities and interests must be considered also. All of this can cause aggravation at a time when it is least possible to deal with because you are not in the frame of mind to do so. Yet, if enough attention is paid to the details in selecting the place to go and consideration is given to each other, a good time can be planned.

Are you willing to leave your children in the care of another person to take a vacation with each other?

For many couples this will not be a simple question that they can quickly answer yes. When you become emotionally involved with children, it is not so simple to leave them. It requires planning and putting up with quite a bit of apprehension even though you have gone on vacation in order to relieve some of the pressures and tensions in your lives.

Yet married couples who have children have a particular need to have some type of vacation in which they spend time together without their children. Mini-vacations can be very pleasing and rewarding in the renewal of your most loving feelings for one another. It is easy to take these for granted or even forget what they are like when you become involved in the everyday routine of marriage, work and children. Simply going away for a weekend to a nearby town may be all that is needed to restore these feelings for one another. This allows you to be nearby in the event that you are needed at home and relieves you from having to drive long distances to get to a vacation spot.

Spending relaxed days with one another and having dinner and entertainment in the evening produces an especially romantic mood and this is all you need as a married couple for renewal of your love for one another. Couples who do not take this time together frequently find that they spend the money other ways that have no beneficial effect on their marriage relationship. Think about it and talk together in order to plan time and money for these mini-vacations for the health of your marriage relationship.

CONCLUSION

Love is the unseen force in life that makes us human. Though we cannot see it, we feel its presence and all of us desire it in our lives. Every person is born with the capability to love and each of us will determine the *degree* and *quality* of the kind of love we want to give and receive.

There are many kinds of love, e.g., love of parents, love of children, love of country, love of our pets and even our car. Love means the giving of self to another person or thing. Some people are able to give more love than others are. Some persons value love in their lives more than others do. There are some adults who want to receive it but are reluctant to give it. These latter ones we call selfish.

As we grow into adulthood we anticipate meeting someone with whom we can "fall in love." At this stage in life most of us want the whole deep sweep of emotion that yearns for a "complete" love. But our yearning for this kind of love can be a trap. Emotions are not always a reliable guide in this business of "falling in love." We need more than emotions to guide us to the person who can give "complete" love to us and to whom we can give the same kind of love in return. Therefore, we need some means of discovering our partner's ability to give us the kind of love we desire.

Love is absolutely essential for meaningful married life to survive. But this kind of love must be combined with knowledge of the person with whom we expect to share our life and love. For love to be true, we must get to "know" the complete person with whom we believe we have "fallen in love."

The many questions in this book should have provoked you to think deeply about yourself and the one person on earth with whom you want the best loving relationship. They were designed to open your minds, your emotions and your spirits to one another so that you will "know" as much about this person as you do about yourself. The questions were not intended to be all-inclusive. Rather, it is hoped that these questions provoked others that are pertinent in your lives and that the analysis they have caused will not stop with the reading of this book, but go on for as long as you live together on earth.

Did you agree with many of the opinions expressed after each question? Did you disagree with some of them? If so, these questions have served their purpose. It is not necessary that you agree with the opinions expressed by the authors, but it is very important that you express your opinions to your partner.

You should have used your analysis of the ideas expressed in your opinions to determine what your moral values are and the status of your maturity. Also analyze whether or not your moral values and the level of your maturity conform closely enough with your partner's for you to give and receive the kind of loving commitment from one another necessary for the quality of married life you are happy to live.

Conclusion

Remember the truism entitled "Can Two Become One?" in the front of this book? If you and your partner are both moral and mature, you will be able to obtain a blend of your love for each other that will result in that unique flavor of marriage – when two become one.

If you have discovered that you are moral and mature and your partner is not, then you won't be able to obtain the kind of love from your partner that will blend your lives together sufficiently to become one in mind, emotion and spirit. But always remember that free will allows you to make the kinds of changes that will bring the two of you close enough to become one.

If you have learned that neither of you are moral and mature then your married lives will be lived on a different level from those who are, and you will never be able to become one as God intended you to be. If you are content in this status, then you will not want to change. If you are not, you must both decide to make changes in your lives that will allow you to love in the manner necessary to become one.

In this book we have tried to show you specifically where to look for the kind of love you want from each other. We have tried to show you how all aspects of your life have affected you and have caused you to be the kind of loving person you offer to your partner and he or she to you.

By now you should be able to quickly answer these questions. Are you able to support yourself? Do you take care of your health? Do you love and respect your parents, your children and your family? Do you attend family reunions and participate in them? Do you give a fair day's work for a day's pay? Do you obey the rules of the road when driving a car? Do you maintain a bad credit rating? Do you respect your name and reputation? The kind of love, the quality that you specifically give to your partner in marriage, will be much the same as you have cultivated the habit of giving to all of these other relationships in your life.

Your love for your partner will be far deeper and more intense than the love shown to any of these, but it will be of a similar degree and quality. How you have loved all of these other people in your life, and how you have inspired them to love you in return, will determine, in great measure, how you love your partner and are able to inspire him or her to love you.

The degree of love in your life is not an unchangeable force. If you want to love with a deeper quality and a more intense passion, you have the free will to learn how to do so. Ordinarily the desire to change comes about by some great motivating force in your life. Your love for one another can provide this motivation. Your free will allows change to occur and permits you to control your destiny. It makes it possible for you to improve the level of your morals and maturity and, therefore, the quality of your love.

Throughout the examination of your attitudes and your opinions regarding your PERSONAL CHARACTER, your FAMILY AND HERITAGE, your RELIGION, your COMMUNITY, your EDUCATION, your CAREER, your HEALTH, and the status of your FINANCES, you were testing the decisions already made by use of your will power. You have arrived at the point you now are in your life and in your marriage as a result of these free will decisions you have made. If you are satisfied with your life and your marriage, then go forward and build your lives together in peace and contentment. If you are not, then change the decisions you have made by exercising the same free will with which you made them.

If you are fortunate enough to go through this analysis before making a commitment to marry, then you can accurately determine the kind of loving commitment you and your partner will be bringing to your marriage.

If you are unhappy in your marriage, it is possibly the result of past decisions, consciously or unconsciously made, that have brought about undesirable consequences. Look to see if these were foreseeable through examining how you and your partner have handled all of your love relationships with others. Use this knowledge to try to affect a change in the way you handle these in the future. It is not necessary that you continue to live with the situation as it is. In some cases it may be intolerable to do so. But, the same free will with which you made former decisions can now change them.

If you are happy in your marriage, enjoying a contented, satisfying life together, then you are already one with each other. Your marriage is a continuing development of your lives together and will go on to more enjoyment and pleasure as years pile upon years.

The analysis that the two of you constantly go through every day of your lives brings you into your partner's mind. As you do this, you discover the emotions that bring forth love in each of you and you will grow to love the spirit that dwells inside your partner. Now it is possible for the two of you to have the greatest relations, physically, that it is possible for two people to share on this earth. You have discovered the miracle in marriage – when two become one.

ADVICE FROM THE AUTHORS

Marriage is the joining of two human beings, with all of the limitations being human implies.

Do not expect perfection in all of your decisions. Try to offset the bad ones with good ones and you will have done a good job.

Do not seek to have the advantages of being single, though married. Give up the freedom of single life and enjoy the privileges of marriage while fulfilling its obligations.

Decide to be moral and mature and realize you cannot be both immoral and immature and moral and mature at the same time. Get the benefits of being moral and mature and accept the limitations.

Don't let an immoral and immature person in your life, and especially do not marry one. If you are married to one use this book to try to educate him or her to become moral and mature. If you cannot, then you may have to live your married life knowing that there is a miracle in marriage that you cannot obtain.

Seek to make all aspects of your lives run smooth. If one part is pulling you down, it will affect all the others.

Do not make enemies of the good people in your lives.

Find some happily married couples as trustworthy models to whom you can turn to for occasional advice.

Be aware that if the person who knows you the best, loves you the most, this indicates you are a truly great person.

Treat each other with the deference, respect and dignity that is due an immortal person,

Love each other outrageously. Dare to walk hand-in-hand in a public park when you are eighty years old.

Achieve the miracle in marriage: Become one and thoroughly enjoy your married lives together on our lovely, fertile, life-supporting planet, Earth – and then – for an Eternity thereafter!

LOVE ME AND I WILL LOVE YOU

By Barbara Del Buono

When you come to me with your love
I'll join you with mine.
We'll blend our lives in one wonderful life
That will be sublime.

I'll see what you see and I'll feel what you feel
As I walk with you.
I'll know what you believe and I'll understand,
And you'll now me too.

Our spirits will soar to the highest heights
As we live our love.
We'll conquer each sorrow that's sure to come
With love from above.

Love me and I will love you
Our whole lives through, Our whole lives through
Love me and I will love you
We're one, though two, We're one though two.

The sheet music for this song is available from:
The Ellingsworth Press, LLC
680 Main Street
Watertown, CT 06795
Toll free: 1- 877 355 7737